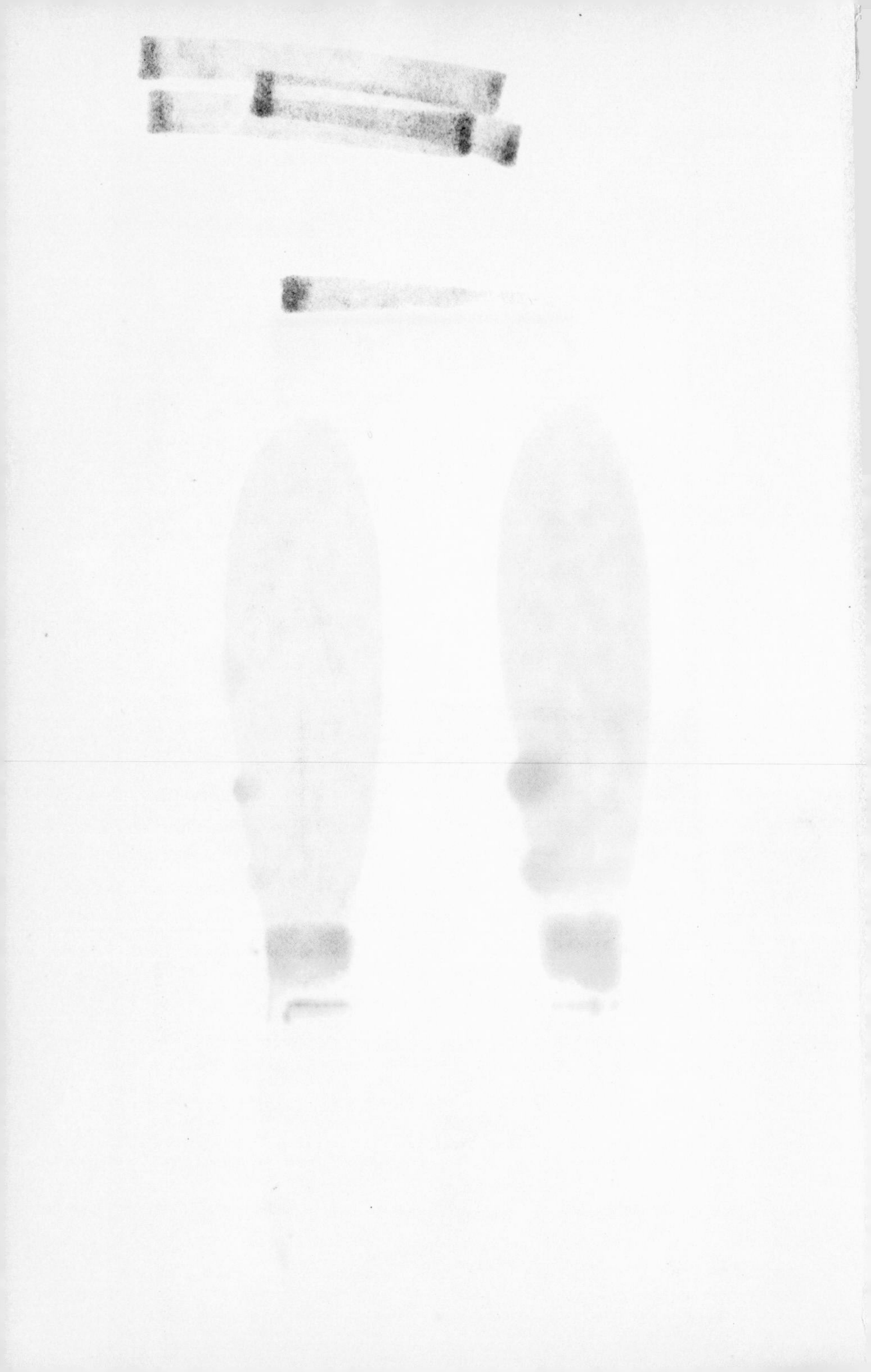

LuLu

LuLu

LuLu Roman

Fleming H. Revell Company
Old Tappan, New Jersey

Unless otherwise identified, Scripture quotations are from the King James Version of the Bible.

Scripture quotations identified LB are from The Living Bible, Copyright © 1971 by Tyndale House Publishers, Wheaton, Illinois 60187. All rights reserved.

Library of Congress Cataloging in Publication Data

Roman, LuLu.
LuLu.

1. Roman, LuLu. 2. Christian biography—United States. 3. Entertainers—United States—Biography. I. Title.
BR1725.R65A34 248'.24 [B] 78-15510
ISBN 0-8007-0956-X

Published by Fleming H. Revell Company

Printed in the United States of America

To Claudine Hable, my beloved grandmother—
who was always there for me, no matter how many times I let her down, no matter how far down I went. Through her faithful and undying love, she bore the shame, the hurt, and the humiliation with her head held high.

I could always run to her, and she never, never left me for any reason. To me, that is the highest example anyone on this earth could give—the example of never-ending patience, a steadfast hope, and an everlasting faith.

To me, she is the world's greatest grandma. She is "my Claudine," and I love her more than words can ever tell.

Contents

Some of the names and events in this book have been changed to protect the persons whose pasts are also a part of my past. For those who are still under bondage, my constant prayer is that the Lord will free them from their burdens as He has freed me.

Our Friend LuLu

LuLu Roman is a special person to me. Through all the years I've known her, she's always been the friendliest "little puppy" of a woman I've ever met. She makes friends wherever she goes, because people can recognize that particular zest for life that she has.

She's had more problems than most, and she's overcome them because life to her is very precious. There's a certain glow that surrounds LuLu nowadays. It's the glow that comes when you know who and what you are—where your life is going. And, I think, her relationship with Christ is responsible for that glow and also her wonderful family.

LuLu's brought joy and happiness to so many people and, as someone who's proud to call her "friend," I'm glad she's found some of that joy for herself.

BUCK OWENS

I remember LuLu from our very first meeting. Anyone would, I suppose, for there's quite a lot to remember.

Over the years, it's been fascinating to see the dramatic and profound changes that have taken place in her life. As a talented, ambitious actress, her career zoomed to the heights and then fell because of what seemed to be insurmountable problems. All of us were saddened by the turn of events in her life that drew her from us.

But—like all beautiful stories—her story as told here will let you share in the experiences that led her finally to a new life of joy—and that brought her back "home" to our "Hee Haw" family and friends.

ROY CLARK

The first things you notice, when you go into her home, are the butterflies. They cling to the draperies, cascade across the walls and perch on the lamps. Butterflies everywhere.

Fashioned of delicate wire, carved in wood, spun from gossamer threads, mounted under glass, embroidered, painted, etched on metal. A breathtakingly beautiful collection, making tinkling notes of color all over the house.

"They're a symbol of immortality," she says, and you know they're more than that. Butterflies are a symbol of LuLu.

Like them, she groveled in the dirt, feeding on earthy, elemental things. Like them, she locked herself away from the lovely things of life, imprisoned in a hard, impenetrable shell.

And like them, she emerged at last, trembling, groping, reaching toward the Light.

Today, she soars, singing God's praises wherever she goes, giving strong words of encouragement to others who are struggling through their own metamorphoses.

This book takes you with her, each step of the way.

DYCIA SAMUELS

This story you will be reading is about a fabulous woman. I've known LuLu Roman for many, many years. I've been agent, manager, and friend to her, and I've listened to and lived with many of her problems. Her story is a fascinating one, and it does have a very happy ending.

An important thing to remember is that LuLu went through all her problems without once losing the great sense of humor that makes her the special type of lady that she is. And when you come to the end of the book, remember, too, that for LuLu, her story is still continuing and in some ways just beginning. She has a very special Someone on her side now—she's found the love of Christ, and she's with her beautiful family. When you watch her on television, you'll see what I see—that her family put back the sparkle in her eyes and that Christ has brought the serenity back into her life.

It's an inspiring story, even more so because it's true, and when you've finished it, I think you'll come to love LuLu just as much as all her friends do.

JACK MC FADDEN

LuLu

1

Everything Had Turned White

I remember that I was very cold and very scared. Granny pulled me behind her out of the car. "I'll be right back," she said to the woman who had brought us here. Then she took my hand and started across the wide driveway toward one of the huge red-brick buildings with their red tile roofs.

I was four years old, and Granny was putting me in the orphanage. I remember that the icy wind seemed to blow right through my little turquoise blue jumper. Even my ears were cold under the pointed white wool hood with the fluffy white pompoms at the end of its strings. I loved that hood, but today it wasn't keeping me warm.

Granny held on firmly as we started up the big white cement steps. She knew my pudgy little legs would have to take them slowly and one at a time. They say it was Einstein who discovered relativity, but I know better. Relativity was discovered by little kids! As I grew older and bigger, those steps grew smaller and smaller until I could run up or down them two at a time.

But on this day everything was very big and very scary.

The next thing I remember was that everything had turned white. There was a white room with a big white wooden bench, and I was sitting on it with my legs dangling over the edge. Granny was standing beside a white desk, talking to a woman who was dressed in all white. A little white cap sat on top of her white coiled hair. I had never seen a nurse before—or anyone else dressed in all white like that—and I thought she was made out of starch. She made me think of the stiff white petticoats Granny used to starch and iron for me.

"Her name is Bertha Louise Hable," Granny was saying, "but we call her Louise."

After some more talk, the starch woman got up from the desk and came over to me. "Come with me, Louise," she said, taking my hand.

"You be a good girl, now," Granny called after me as we started down the hall.

The starch woman took me into a smaller room where another starch woman was waiting. She put me on the edge of a high white cot and told me to stick out my tongue. She looked into my eyes and ears and checked my head for lice. She took my temperature, weighed and measured me, and tapped my knee with a little hammer that made my foot jerk. She took off my clothes, pressed my skin in several spots, and then she turned me over her knee and checked my bottom for worms.

After that, the first starch woman dressed me again and took me into another long white room where a whole bunch of kids was playing and making a lot of noise. Another one of those starch women was sitting at a desk in a corner. She got up and came toward us, and the two women talked. Then the new starch woman took my hood away and handed me a big pink doll.

"Here, Louise," she said, "you can play with this." I started to, but a boy came over and tried to take the doll away from me. I pushed him down on the floor and pulled the doll away from him. "She'll be all right," the new starch woman said, and the first one went out of the room.

Some scenes stand out in my mind, fading in and out of one another the way things do in a dream. After that episode, I don't remember anything else until bedtime.

There was a long white room with eight or ten little white beds in it. I was sitting on one of them while the starch women came down the aisle, helping everyone get ready for bed. Finally one of them laid a pair of little white pajamas on the white bedspread and started to untie my shoe. "It's time to get ready for bed," she said, but I pulled my foot away and shouted, "No! I'm going home with Granny."

"Your grandmother has gone home," the starch woman said. "She said good-bye to you; don't you remember? You're going to stay here with us now."

I didn't believe her. Granny had left me with a sitter while she went shopping sometimes, but she always came for me before nightfall. I wouldn't believe she wasn't coming back. And besides, I knew the sitter—but these starch women were strangers. I kicked and struggled, but when one turned me over and spanked me, I knew she meant business, and I let her put me to bed.

For a long time, I lay there sobbing with the blankets pulled over my head because, before she went away, the starch woman had said, "If you make a sound, I'll blister your bottom!" I was frightened, sick to my stomach with loneliness, and shivering because I had to go to the bathroom. When I woke up in the morning, the bed was wet, and I got another spanking.

In looking back, I know my Granny did what she thought was best for me. She was really my great-grandmother. My grandmother, I called Claudine. My mother had been ill since shortly after I was born, and these two were doing the best for me that they could. But they wrangled over me constantly. Claudine said Granny was too strict with me, and Granny said Claudine spoiled me.

Granny was hard-core Methodist with an unyielding fanaticism about cleanliness and godliness and a thou-shalt-not approach to both. "Thou shalt not get thy dress dirty, nor thy hands, nor thy elders' sheets and towels." I can still remember being sent back to the washbasin four and five times until my hands would pass inspection.

When I was little, the godliness part meant grace at meals and "Now I lay me down to sleep" at bedtime. I was one of the uncounted horde of little children who suffered untold horrors in the night over that one, especially the part that says, "If I should die before I wake . . . ." That and the gory pictures in our big Bible of Herod's men beheading tiny babies and little children being thrown alive into the fiery mouth of Baal terrified me.

Sunday was the Lord's Day and the *thou shalt nots* were even worse. "Thou shalt not play with thy toys. Thou shalt not watch TV, except for church programs. Thou shalt not enjoy thyself"—period! I was given a special scrub-down on Saturday night. On Sunday morning I put on my Sunday dress and my Sunday shoes and went to Sunday school and church. The pews were hard and uncomfortable. The minister droned on and on, and I fidgeted or fell asleep. I liked it best when I fell asleep.

After dinner (always served at noon), I was allowed to dry the silverware when Granny washed the dishes. Then I could watch religious programs on television or look at religious picture books. If some of Granny's friends from church dropped in, we had cake and tea.

Claudine was never around on Sundays. Somewhere in her youth, she had rebelled against all this and had gone off on her own. Claudine smoked. She painted her face and tinted her hair and wore slacks—and I adored her. She played games with me and bought me everything she had always wanted when she was a child and was never allowed to have. She had no small talk and nothing in common with any of Granny's church friends, so when Sunday rolled around, Claudine disappeared, but I missed her longingly.

Granny looked after me because she considered it to be her Christian duty, but she often said she was too old for it. My noise and constant activity irritated her, and she was always yelling at me for getting dirt on my hands or clothing. But she was good to me in her own way. She baked cookies for me, and pie and coffee cake and cinnamon rolls. And, somehow, she never seemed to realize that all her "goodness" was making me pudgier and pudgier.

Then an article in the local paper nudged the course of my life into a different direction. The police were combing our neighborhood, the article said, for a transient who had abused two little girls in a park just a couple of blocks from us. When Granny read that, she went into immediate action. Without a word to Claudine, she packed me up, clothes and all, and took me to the Home. She knew it would be easier to tell Claudine about it after it was done.

Granny knew about the Home through her church friends and her minister. They had told her that children got a good education there because it was run by God-fearing people.

The pastors I remember tried their best to make us God-fearing people, too, but I have often wondered what it might have been like if they had tried to instill a *love* for God in us instead.

2

Whistles and Bells

As I grew older, I learned that the all-white building with its white starch women was the receiving area or welcome center. It was the place where we were kept for a few days to be sure we didn't have any diseases and where they let us work off our homesickness and learn how to get along with the other children. After a week or so, we were taken to the dormitory where the preschoolers lived.

Sometimes I think the man who wrote Ecclesiastes must have lived at the Home because it, too, had a "time for everything." Only at the Home, time was all marked off with whistles and bells. There were whistles to get up, bells to get washed and dressed, whistles and bells to march to the dining hall, for work and for play, for sports and for school, and even a buzzing bell for "lights out" instead of a loving "good-night."

I don't remember a great deal about the preschool dorm, except that our lives seemed to be regulated by the whistles and bells and centered on learning and obeying the rules. If we broke a rule, we weren't likely to do it again, because punishment was swift and sure and serious. The only psychology was the kind they applied right to the seat of the difficulty!

Until I came to the Home, there hadn't been any children for me to play with except in Sunday school. None of Granny's or

Claudine's friends had little children, so I didn't have any playmates and had really never been exposed to other girls or boys. After I had been at the Home for a while, I was playing in the sandbox with some of the other children one day when one of the little boys suddenly decided it was either too far or too late to get up and go all the way indoors to the bathroom. So he pulled down his elastic-topped trousers and made a little puddle right there in the sand.

Well, now! That was different! I didn't have anything like that (at least I didn't think I did), and while I was checking to make sure, he discovered that little girls are different. The whole incident would have passed over and been forgotten long ago, except that right then one of the teachers happened to look our way. My first whipping with a long strip of linoleum is something I'll never forget.

There were other things I'll never forget either. Like the can with a long thin spout that they put under the sheet with me whenever I choked up and couldn't breathe. As a child, I couldn't understand why that happened, but every once in a while I seemed to run out of air. I'd gasp and wheeze but couldn't seem to get air into my lungs. At those times, they'd put me in bed with a sheet over my head and the can with the long spout beside me. A kind of mist came out of it that smelled sort of medicinal, but after a minute or so it helped me to breathe again, and I didn't mind it.

The earlier years in the Home have grown hazy in my memory, but I remember there were fun times, too. We had a big play yard in back of our building with swings and teeterboards and slides, and we used to have a screaming time playing games and splashing in the sprinklers.

Then one day the long-awaited time came, and I was old enough to start school and to move into the first-grade girls' dorm! I can still remember how grown-up I felt, carrying my clothes and possessions across the grass and up the stairs to the top floor of my "new" building. At the Home, we started on the top floor and worked our way down. As the seniors graduated and moved away each year, the juniors and sophomores moved down a floor, making room at the top for a new group of students. And all across the campus the same kind of reshuffling was going on.

Beds were stripped. Mattresses were turned and aired. Closets were emptied and all the stuff you had accumulated through the year was sorted out or carefully carried to the place you would occupy until next moving day came along.

The preschool dorm I had moved out of was more like one huge ward with beds around three sides of it. The housemothers kept a watchful eye on everything from the center of the room. Now I found myself in a much smaller room with eight beds in it and a line of closets along one wall where we put our clothes. One of the older girls helped me put my things away and make up my bed. I remember going to the window to look down from that third floor and feeling a little dizzy at the height.

The Home was very much like a small city, situated on two square blocks of space. The two- and three-story red-brick buildings with their red tile roofs were built around the edge of the square. The administration building was in the center of one side of the square, with the church and Sunday-school room on its top floor. Directly behind it on the opposite side of the square was the Mart, or commissary, with the clothing store above. On the one side of the square were the girls' dormitories, the kitchen, dining hall, hospital, and laundry. On the other side were the boys' dorms, the tool shops, vocational building, machine shop, and so on.

There were wide grassy areas separating the buildings, and I remember that whenever one of the boys got sick and had to go to the hospital, he'd have to walk across the grass, past the girls' dorms. Then we'd all hang out the windows to gawk at him and snicker.

Inside each of the girls' dorms there were two or three rooms like a small apartment for each of the housemothers and there were living-room areas with couches, desks, and tables where we could do our homework. Some of the dorms had pianos, and I think one or two of them had fireplaces and all of them had televisions—but nothing looked homelike or pretty or inviting. The floors were gray cement or gray linoleum with no rugs or carpets. The windows had yellowing shades but no drapes. The furniture was functional, drab, and, for the most part, uncomfortable.

The bedrooms were all painted a sickish pea green with floors and bedspreads of the same icky color. The baths were a community affair, with basins all in a row and stall showers with curtains. In one corner of the floor there was a square tile basin where we washed our feet.

Only our clothes closets afforded a sense of privacy or personal ownership. These were a line of tall wooden cubicles about four feet deep and four feet wide, built from floor to ceiling along one wall. They had drawers and shelves and a bar for hanging dresses and coats. There was barely room enough to turn around in them and no place to sit except on the floor, but if you wanted to get away from the prying eyes of your roommates, that's where you went. And, anyway, the shelves were *yours* to arrange exactly as you pleased, to show off your trinkets and souvenirs and the photos of your favorite movie stars as you got older. I remember hauling pictures of Andy Williams and Natalie Wood from floor to floor and from building to building. And I remember getting into some screaming hair-pulling matches with a couple of girls who wanted to steal them.

But for the most part, my days in the elementary grades were spent in trying to conform to the rules and stay out of trouble. In an institution where the emphasis was on following the rules, there was no incentive—and far too much risk—to try to be different. But I was a very expressive child, with eyes and facial contortions that said a great deal too much without my need to utter a word, and I was constantly getting into trouble without even trying. Many times, if I just reared back and looked at a housemother when she was scolding me, I'd hear, "Don't you buck those eyes at me!"—and I'd get switched with one of those linoleum strips. Or paddled—they had thick wooden paddles with round holes cut into them that raised big welts on your body when they spanked you with them. For milder insurrections you'd have to scrub and wax floors or pull weeds or wash windows.

The worst punishment they had was to make you "sit on the

wall.'' This one, I think, was dreamed up for some kind of torture chamber. We had to stand with our backs against the wall, then slide down until we were in a sitting position, and stay there for half an hour or so with our hands on our knees. I can remember ten or fifteen of us little kids ''sitting on the wall'' that way with our little legs just trembling. If we fell down, we'd have to get back up, and they'd start timing all over again.

And one time, one of the girls in my room got into some kind of trouble and got a horrible beating. One of the housemothers sat her on the bed with her legs between the iron bars at the end and held her there while another housemother beat her with one of those wooden paddles to ''break her will.''

We didn't have to see more than one or two of those disciplinary measures to make up our minds to stay out of trouble, and staying out of trouble meant getting into the routine and following the rules.

The routine was easy. It was all marked off for us by those whistles and bells. They started with four or five short whistles at 5:30 A.M. That was for the older kids who had kitchen work to do. There was a rising bell to get us out of bed. We washed and got dressed and, if it was raining, we put on our slickers and boots. There was a warning whistle that sent us outside to line up in front of our dorms, and then another whistle that sent us marching two by two to the dining hall.

They called it Manna Hall for ''manna from heaven,'' but to me it seemed to be called that because the food was always the same. We could tell what day of the week it was just by looking at the food on our plates. Monday: chicken loaf, Tuesday: chipped beef, Wednesday: chili, and so on. The chili always had two or three inches of grease floating on top, and we'd have to strain the vegetables up through the grease. We could get it down all right if it was piping hot, but when the chili started to get cold, the grease would congeal, and then it was awful. And with it we always had sliced bananas with a dab of whipped cream on top or cantaloupe when it was in season.

They used to bring melons to us in great big trucks, and the men who unloaded them always managed to drop a few oversized watermelons so they'd split open when they hit the ground. Then, after they drove away, we'd dash out there like a flock of hungry sparrows and have a watermelon feast.

Sometimes we'd have a pork chop or a small piece of steak, but it was never the treat it should have been because it was always served to us half raw. On Saturdays we always had red beans and corn bread, and on Sundays we had fried chicken—singed on the outside, bloody next to the bone. To this day I won't eat meat at all unless it's very well done.

It seems as if there were hundreds of long tables in Manna Hall. We marched around our tables and stood behind our chairs while someone played the piano. The pastor or superintendent or a housemother would come to the microphone on the platform in the center of the room and say grace. Then we all sat down, and the babble and clatter began.

There were six girls at each table, with a housemother at one end and an older girl who served as our waitress at the other. I can still remember how I used to look up to those girls and how I always tried to sit next to them so I could ask questions. Then one day it was my turn to be waitress, and the littler kids were looking up to me.

The waitresses went to the kitchen and brought back huge bowls of food and pitchers of milk and served each of us individually. There was always plenty of food, and I can't remember ever going hungry. There was a rule that you had to eat everything on your plate. Finickiness about food was simply not tolerated at the Home. You ate what was in front of you, or you sat there until you did. If you were still sitting there when everyone else was through and gone, you were punished.

The boys ate at separate tables—so I didn't see this happen, but I heard my best friend, Patty, tell about it many times. Like myself, Patty was not a real orphan. Very few kids at the Home were. Most came from broken homes or families that for some reason or other were unable to take care of them. All four of the children in Patty's family were there, and her mother worked there for a while until frustration and helplessness over situations she could do nothing about finally caused a breakdown.

Patty's little brother was only five when he came to the Home. He had what was called a "nervous stomach" and may have been allergic to eggs, but *allergy* was a word that had not yet infiltrated the Home. Any failure to comply was simply treated as willful disobedience and handled accordingly. So, when the little fellow tried to eat the eggs that were set before him and had to run outside and throw up, they spanked him and brought him back and went through the whole thing all over again. Then, when his whole upset emotional condition caused him to wet the bed at night, they punished him again.

I remember that Patty's mother always seemed rather sad and often had tears in her eyes, but it wasn't until I became a mother myself that I really understood why.

I was always a very lonely child, and Patty's mother was very good to me. She cooked for some of the staff and once in a while, when they were away, she took us up to her rooms and cooked fried chicken or some other treat for us. She knew we didn't get the same kind of food that the directors did. I suppose now I would think of her as apperceptive, but at that time I knew only that she was gentle and very kind.

We were walking across the campus one evening on the way to her rooms when I spotted a fuzzy, crawly thing in the grass ahead of me. I raised my foot to squash it, but she stopped me and pulled me away.

"Please don't step on it," she said. "Give it a chance to become what it's supposed to be."

"But it's only an ugly old worm," I protested.

"It may appear to be ugly," she said, "but remember, you learned in Sunday school that Jesus taught us not to judge by appearances. That 'worm' as you call it is really a caterpillar, and if you give it a chance to grow and unfold the way God intended it to, your 'ugly old worm' will turn into a beautiful butterfly."

In addition to Patty's mother, there were some housemothers and a couple of nurses at the hospital who were very kind to me. Occasionally they would let me sit with them in the evenings and watch television while they sewed or ironed. I'd tell them about my hopes and hurts, and sometimes they'd let me make fudge or popcorn. And, as I grew older, one of the housemothers even let me bake pecan pies for her.

Granny's church friends had been right about one thing—we did get a good education at the Home. When we left there, we were well qualified to start off on two or three different vocations. I studied typing for six years and home economics for seven and was really a whiz at both. So, when I learned to bake pecan pies, this particular housemother let me do my "homework" in her oven. But while I became more roly-poly than ever, she never seemed to put on an ounce.

She was tall and thin and majestic, with silver hair done up in a roll on top of her head. She wore glasses and had a very stern countenance. Only, her heart was soft and tender. When I was sick with measles or chicken pox or anything else that was contagious and kept me in the isolation ward, she always came to see me and brought me little treats. Her visits—and getting to watch television while the other kids were in school—made sick time almost a delight to experience.

Sometimes I think these particular housemothers felt sorry for me because I was always such a pudgy and awkward youngster and the other girls excluded me from their little groups and cliques. I had always been somewhat of an attention getter, and this kind of treatment only made me try harder to win the girls' approval. So I did things to make them laugh such as making faces behind the teachers' backs or trying to balance a glass of water on my head. Naturally, all this clowning invariably got me into trouble.

There was no psychology, as such, used at the Home. There were no attempts at teaching us personal or social relationships except for the Southern Baptist version of the Bible, which seemed at that time to be little more than a vast theology of *thou shalt nots*. But thou shalt notting didn't win me any friends, and I was starved for relationships with other young people, for a sense of belonging and being wanted. Consequently when a housemother took pity on me and showed a little extra consideration, I turned myself inside out to win her approval so I would be allowed to watch her television or sit and talk with her while she did her work.

Of course, this only alienated me from my roommates all the more. "P.C.," they used to say, which stood for "Privileged Character," or "Teacher's Pet." And they'd gang up in a corner and whisper and giggle and make me feel more rejected and left out than ever. So I'd go off by myself and mope in a corner or go out in front of the dorm and hang by my knees from a limb of my favorite tree, until someone came along and said, "Little ladies don't act like tomboys!"

Weekdays were so regimented that it seemed they were all cut out of the same piece of cloth. We got up at the rising bell, marched to Manna Hall for breakfast, went to school, marched to Manna Hall for lunch, went back to school, went to our dorms and washed up, marched to Manna Hall for supper, did our homework, and went to bed. If we got our homework done, we could watch an hour or so of television. If we didn't have too much homework, we could romp around outdoors in our play yard for a while.

About the only variation from one day to the next during the week was the food served to us each day, and I guess one of the deep, underlying reasons why I still like red beans and corn bread so much is because at the Home they were always associated with an "Oh, wow! It's Saturday!" feeling.

Saturdays were different. On Saturdays, we had free time. On Saturdays we could play outdoors in the play yard or just sit under a tree and dream if we wanted to. There were also certain times of the day when we could take our allowance and go to the Mart and squander it on licorice whips, caramels, gumdrops and all those other wonderful goodies they kept in big glass jars.

Although there were fifteen hundred kids in the Home, they managed to give us each a weekly allowance. We got ten cents a week when we were little, twenty-five cents a week about junior-high-school age, and fifty cents a week in high school. Of course, relatives used to give us spending money, also. I used to take my allowance and trudge over to the Mart and spend it on candy. I always got the penny-a-piece kinds, because that way I'd have some for every day of the week until I could go to the Mart again, and I'd also have some for trading with the other girls or for "buying" favors.

I learned very early that a piece of candy, a hair ribbon, or some other trinket could "buy" me a little friendship—sometimes for a whole day.

In looking back, I realize there had to be some kind of regimentation at the Home, or with that many kids, everything would have fallen into complete chaos. If some of the staff seemed harsh or overzealous in punishing us, the percentage was probably no greater than it would have been at any other institution. I also believe they tried to give us every advantage they could, and it really wasn't their fault if we blew it. Take, for example, piano lessons.

Even as a small child, I loved music. Whenever we sang in church or in school or in the auditorium, my voice could be heard above all the rest. It was high and squeaky and often off-key, but I had lots of lung power. So, when they offered to give piano lessons to the kids who were interested, I asked my housemother to let me sign up.

Everything went along fine with the lessons for a while. The piano teacher was young and pretty and kind, and I adored her. There were several practice rooms above the auditorium with a piano in each. I was assigned to one of the rooms at a certain time each Saturday morning. I was working very hard and making quite a bit of progress when one of my roommates was assigned to the next room at the same time. That's when my old adversary—the craving for attention—came on the scene.

My roommate, Cory, was a very pretty and popular girl, petite and blue eyed, with curly blond hair she wore in a pixie cut. She had the prettiest dresses, the largest dolls, and the most presents from relatives of any girl in our room, and I wanted desperately to be one of her friends, so I could be part of the little clique that hung around her.

I tried to gain Cory's admiration by showing her how well I had practiced, but that little scheme went right down the drain. Cory had taken piano lessons before she came to the Home. She zipped through the scales effortlessly while my lumbering fingers were still trying to work in unison. I was crushed, and the next time I went home to Granny's house, I told Claudine all about it.

The kids who had friends or relatives to come and get them were allowed to leave the Home for two or three Saturdays a month, just as long as we were back again by 5:30 in the evening. Before I started the piano lessons, I used to go to the window right after breakfast on Saturday mornings and stand there with my nose pressed against the glass, waiting for the first sight of Granny and Claudine driving up in their car. The moment I saw them coming through the gate, I used to fly down the stairs and rush to the street, usually getting to the parking area before they had a chance to open the door.

There was never very much to do at Granny's. When Claudine was home, she'd take me shopping, and we usually stopped for lunch in the coffee shop at the hotel where she worked. I loved that. Claudine let me have whopping big hot-fudge sundaes for dessert. If she was working, I'd just sit at home in Granny's rocker, watching television or reading and stuffing myself with Granny's homemade cookies or fresh-baked cinnamon buns.

I was contented just to be away from the Home for a while, but I was happiest when Claudine was there. Granny used to yell at me for tracking in mud or dirtying my dress or getting cookie crumbs on the carpet. But if she was strict with me, Claudine leaned just as far in the other direction. She used to spoil me by letting me use her bubble bath and cologne. She'd cut my hair in attractive ways and let me practice manicuring my fingernails.

Claudine never seemed like a grandmother to me. She was young and attractive with reddish hair and dark blue eyes, and she always dressed up to date. Grandmothers, I thought, were old and white haired and crotchety. Claudine wasn't anything like that at all. She was my pal, my older sister, my confidante. I poured out all my hurts and secrets to her, like this latest fret over Cory.

"Huh!" she snorted in response to my tale of woe, "all we have to do is find some way to get one up on her."

Sure, Claudine. Like what? Everything I had, Cory had in multiples of two or three. Everything I could do, she could do better. Just how did she think I was going to get ahead of Cory?

But when I told Patty about it later that evening, she had what seemed like a very bright idea. Right after Sunday dinner next day, she skipped the only chance she'd have all week to talk with her brothers and sneaked up to the practice room with me instead. Then over and over again, we practiced "Chopsticks" until I could play it perfectly.

I couldn't wait to show Cory, so the very first chance I had, I lured her up to the practice room and performed my two-fingered concerto for her.

"That's pretty good," Cory said. Then she slid onto the piano bench next to me and played the bass accompaniment—with boogie-woogie variations. Even though she stayed with me until we were turning out a pretty creditable performance, I was still chagrined and crestfallen. But that night while I was lying in bed wide awake and thinking about it, I had an idea.

For several days, while the other girls were watching TV or studying, I slipped over to the practice room and worked on my stunt. When I was sure I could do it without any mistakes, I told Cory I had something to show her over there and got her to come to the practice room with me.

"This is a very difficult exercise," I told her solemnly. "None of the great composers like Chopin or Liszt was able to do this." Then I took off my shoes and bobby socks, laid down on my back on the piano bench and played "Chopsticks" with my bare toes.

Cory screamed with laughter. "That's fun-nee!" she howled. "Please teach me how to do it."

I was in seventh heaven. At last I could do something that she couldn't do. I don't know whether my feet were more agile or whether my toes were longer or what it was, but Cory wasn't nearly as good at it as I was, and I was gloating with glee. We were lying there on the bench and I was magnanimously showing her just how to arch her back and bend her toes when the door opened and Mrs. Ridgeley walked in.

There were housemothers whom I adored and housemothers

whom I respected and stood a little in awe of, but I was *afraid* of Mrs. Ridgeley. I used to have nightmares about her in which her teeth were like fangs and her fingers were long and gnarled and green and she chased me with a huge butcher knife or a sword.

Actually it was her nose that was pointed. She was a tall, masculine woman with straight, short black hair, a nasal voice, and beady black eyes that seemed to bore right through you. Stamping across the room, she grabbed us each by an arm and hauled us off the bench, then almost dragged us out into the hall. I don't know how hard she was holding onto Cory, but my arm had a black-and-blue mark for several days afterward. Out in the hall, she gave us both a yank that almost jerked us off our feet. "Don't you dare, don't you ever dare, go *near* that room again," she snarled, and thus ended my piano lessons.

I still regret the incident, because I would like very much to play the piano today.

When I was little, I used to think that one of the worst things that could possibly happen was for it to rain on Saturdays. Whenever I heard a weather report on the radio or television that said we were going to have rain on Saturday, I used to pray about it. "Please, God, don't let it rain Saturday. That's the only day we have any fun. Let it rain on Sunday or some other day, please!" And I can remember standing at the window on the Saturdays when God didn't hear me and it was pouring outside. I used to stand there and chant that old ditty, "Rain, rain go away, come again some other day," with all the concentrated effort of a full-fledged sorceress, because—once in a while—it seemed to work. The rain would ease up after a while, and before long the sun would come out, and I was always *sure* it was my chanting that had done it.

But on the days when it didn't work, there was always the problem of what to do inside. The girls who had pen pals used to write long letters to them, and the girls who had relatives used to write short letters or postcards, but the rest of us used to get bored. We'd work on our scrapbooks, wash our socks and underwear and hang them on the steam radiators to dry, shampoo our hair, and get into mischief.

Sometimes we'd haul everything out of our closets onto the floor and exchange closets with one another. Sometimes we'd get into the older girls' closets and have a snickering, giggling, hysterical time hooking up their bras and sanitary belts over our clothes and parading around the room in them. Or, if we were really desperate for something to do, we'd go into the bathroom and use our toothpaste to paint our faces like clowns. Then we'd make paper hats out of sacks or newspaper and pretend we were putting on a circus. One time, I was lining up the "animals" and handling the lights for such a pretend circus when the pretend ringmaster called, "Lights," and I was supposed to turn on the lights. Instead of turning the switch on, I let fly with my foot and tried to kick it on and kicked the whole switch right off the wall. Instead of sitting down to supper that night, I ate mine standing up, and I had to sleep on my stomach, too. I still didn't feel very much like sitting down the next day, either, even though I had to in Sunday school and church.

But what hurt worst of all was missing the movies on Saturday night. I stayed in the dorm, because they wouldn't let me stand up in the auditorium during the show.

We had movies or speakers on Saturday evenings, and even though they were old westerns or young seminarians, they were the only big event of the week to which we really looked forward. Once in a rare while, we had a Disney movie, or once in a rarer while, we had a real live movie actor come and talk to us. I even polished my shoes for those occasions.

On Sundays, we went to church—morning and evening. And in the afternoons we rested, because Sunday was the Lord's day, and the Bible said that on the seventh day, God rested.

I can remember how confusing that was to me when I first started to learn about calendars. We went to Sunday school and church on Sunday, and we rested on Sunday, because Sunday was the Lord's day. But, on the calendar, Sunday was the first day of the week, and in Sunday school, they taught us that God rested on the seventh day. I couldn't understand that, but when I questioned it, they thought I was being smart and made me "sit on the wall."

There was another time when the question came up about God's resting on Sunday, but I had started high school by that time, and I was no longer afraid to ask questions of my teacher.

A very large, new high school had been built in our area, and they took us there by bus instead of our finishing our schooling at the Home. We were studying biology at the time, and our teacher was impressing upon us how wonderfully and wisely God had made everything, including the human body. He showed us motion pictures and slides to illustrate the precision and order of the universe and how many light years it would take to get to the nearest star. He discussed the instinct and intelligence of animals and the responsiveness of plants. He showed us that even the tiniest insect, so small we could hardly see it, had organs of sensory perception that served it just as well as our eyes, ears, nose, and taste buds served us. And then he showed us how powerless we would be to keep even an infinitesimal part of all this functioning by our own initiative and understanding.

Right in the middle of being overwhelmed by the magnitude and magnificence of it all, another awesome thought struck me. "Oh, wow!" I said aloud. "We'd sure be in one heck of a fix if God really rested on Sunday."

Of course, everyone laughed, but I was dead serious. And I still needed an answer to my question. I felt very keenly that all the things I had just seen and learned about God's handiwork were true. But I had been taught that, as the Word of God, the Bible was true also, and this seemed to be a contradiction. This time, I was determined to solve the riddle by getting some straight answers from my teacher.

Mr. Meineke was a medium-sized man with salt-and-pepper hair and clear brown eyes that always seemed to have a light behind them. His hands fascinated me. He had slender, tapering fingers that moved over and around objects almost as if he were caressing them. I never heard him raise his voice, and I never saw anyone get out of line in his class. He had a way of imparting knowledge that made us want to be there.

He was on his way out of the room at recess time when I cornered him with my question. "Mr. Meineke, is there any way that the universe can run on its own without God?"

"No, Louise," he said, "there isn't. Why?"

"Well," I blurted, "out at the Home they make us rest on Sundays, because the Bible says God rested on Sunday, but from what I've been learning lately, it seems to me that the whole universe would fall apart if God didn't do exactly the same on Sunday as He does all the rest of the week. Doesn't the Bible mean what it says?"

Motioning me to a seat, he took a big brown book labeled *The Synonym Finder* from his desk and sat down beside me. "Yes," he said, "the Bible means what it says. But our problem isn't in what the Bible means, our problem is in what people think it means." He pushed the book in front of me and told me to open it to the word *rest*.

"You see," he said, pointing to the column of words underneath it, "there are all these different meanings for the word *rest* and sometimes, especially if you're translating from one language to another, it's difficult to tell exactly which meaning was intended. The Old Testament was written in Hebrew before it was translated into English, and in the verse where it says God rested, the word *shabath* was used which also has several meanings. One of those meanings is 'to cease,' and another one is 'to celebrate.' Don't you suppose," he continued with a twinkle in his eye, "that when God finally finished creating the universe and everything in it, He might have felt like celebrating?"

"Whew!" I laughed, "I guess so. But do you believe God really rests on Sundays?"

"No, Louise, I don't," he said. "I believe that when the Bible says God rested, in this instance, it means that He had finished His labors. I don't believe it means that He fell asleep."

3

Worst Days/Best Days

But at the Home, we rested on Sundays—literally—for a couple of hours in the afternoon.

After breakfast, we went to Sunday school and then to church. We came back from church and went to Manna Hall for Sunday dinner, our big meal of the day. Most of the time it was fried chicken—fried on the outside and red on the inside. About the only time that it was cooked so we could enjoy it was when we had visitors or at Homecoming.

On one such occasion, Patty's little brother got into trouble over it. As he and the other boys were filing out of Manna Hall after dinner, he looked up at one of the visitors and said, "I want to thank you, sir, for being here today. That's the best meal we've had in a long time." When Patty told me about it, I laughed. Until she told me how her little brother had been severely punished for his innocent remark and how her mother had cried and cried.

Another time, one of the older boys looked at a piece of half-raw chicken on his plate and said, "I've seen chickens get well when they weren't wounded any worse than this." The boys around him laughed so loud that he had to stand up and tell what he had said. Then they made him run the gauntlet. The other boys formed two lines and took off their belts. He had to run between the lines, stripped to the waist, while they lashed him with their belts as he ran through.

If you had visitors on Sundays, you could go to the welcome center and visit with them for an hour after Sunday dinner. If you had brothers or sisters in the Home, you could meet them at the Circle and talk for a while or run around and play. The Circle was in the center of the large square formed by all the buildings. It was actually five circles, one inside the other. In the very center, there was a large statue of the founder of the Home. A circle of bushes grew around that with a low cement wall forming another circle outside the bushes. Then there was a wide grassy circle, and outside that, a circular parking area for staff cars. Boys and girls who had crushes on each other would go there too on Sundays and pretend they were brothers and sisters—until they got caught.

A warning signal would blow signaling that it was time for the visitors to leave. Then another whistle would blow and that meant everyone had to go to their dorms to rest. We had to lie on our beds and not talk or whisper or stir around. When we got older, we were allowed to read, but when we were little, we were supposed to take naps.

Then we'd get up after a couple of hours and have supper in our dorms. No one worked on Sundays any more than absolutely necessary, not even in the kitchen. They fixed box suppers for us and brought them to the dorms ahead of time. Sandwiches, potato chips, a piece of fruit, and a couple of cookies or a piece of cake.

On Sunday evenings we went back to church for Training Union. It was a repetition of Sunday school except that it was mostly Bible study and prayers with very little singing. I still don't know why they called it Training Union though, because there was no union of any kind involved, and I couldn't see that we were being trained for anything either. Like so many things at the Home, it was something we did because it was part of the regime, but no one ever explained how it applied to us personally.

For example, "health" lectures were given to us at puberty. A public-health nurse came and showed us a film about growing from childhood to womanhood, but it was a very general thing with no specific instruction. It was something that happened to "girls," but when it actually happened to me, I was terrified. I had sat there, listening to the words and looking at the pictures without having any idea of how it affected *me*.

For the most part, our religious training was like that, too. It all seemed to have happened a very long time ago in places that were very far away. I didn't see how any of it applied to me, in this generation, except perhaps for the Golden Rule and the Ten Commandments.

I had memorized John 3:16, along with a hundred or so other Bible verses, but I didn't understand it. "For God so loved the world, that he gave his only begotten Son . . . ." I wouldn't even let the other girls play rough with my doll, and I was very sure that if I ever had a real baby, I wouldn't let anyone hurt it. How could God let the only child He ever had be crucified for people He didn't even know, for people who hadn't even been born yet?

I remembered the picture in Granny's big Bible of little children being thrown into the awful, gaping, fiery mouth of the huge idol. Those people were called heathen and evil, but why were they "bad" for sacrificing their children, when God was supposed to be loving for sacrificing His only child?

Actually, I didn't like Sunday school or church. Most of the teachers seemed far more interested in maintaining discipline than they were in making the lesson material interesting, and I didn't care much about coloring pictures or making little paper toys.

Our pastor didn't help the situation any, either. He was a thickset, balding little man with a very loud voice. He wore a pin-striped coat and a black bow tie, and when he wanted to emphasize a point, he shook his finger at us and slapped his pockets which made all his loose change jingle.

When I was little, I took his sermons quite literally which either caused me to be ridiculed by the older children or made me lie awake at night, wet with cold sweat and terrified at the thought of dying.

I remember one time when his sermon was on Ecclesiastes 11:1: "Cast thy bread upon the waters: for thou shalt find it after many days." Very carefully I dropped half a slice of bread into my lap at lunchtime, then managed to slide it into my pocket unobserved. During playtime, I ran down to the bulrush pond and threw the bread out on the water. Three days later, I went back and was looking for it in the rushes when two older girls walked past. They asked what I was looking for, and I told them, but instead of explaining, they just laughed at me. I was in eighth grade before I understood the figurative meaning for that verse.

The church was on the top floor of the administration building which was the central building located on one side of the huge square of buildings that comprised the Home. The ground floor of the administration building doubled as a theater for our movies on Saturday nights and as an auditorium for speakers, slide programs, or other events. The Sunday-school rooms were used for classrooms and for Vacation Bible School in summer. And for one glorious week in summer, we went to Bible camp at Lake Lavonne.

I loved it! I loved the trees and the lake and the outdoor campfires, and most of all, I loved the singing. It was a singing camp. You'd hear kids walking through the woods, singing; or out on the lake in canoes, singing; or harmonizing in the halls, humming in the showers, singing rounds and descants on the trails; or singing grace at meals and good-night songs in the evening.

Of course it all added up to a giant revival meeting, and there were young students from the seminary who talked to us every evening about our need to be saved, but I didn't mind their talks. Once in a while, there would be one who read his whole talk, or someone who seemed artificial and "put on," but on the whole they were sincere young men who got right down to the nitty-gritty of everyday problems in living.

I was deeply moved by the things they said and made all kinds of resolutions to really live my life for the Lord, but when I got back to the Home, it all melted away again. I thought a lot about going forward when the invitation was given, but I couldn't get up nerve enough to walk all the way down to the front past all those rows and rows of kids.

The Bible students lived right with us at camp. They acted as our leaders and counselors, and it was a joy to have them with us.

Their understanding and patience and their loving-kindness in everything made Jesus seem very real and very close. I've often thought that if they could have lived with us at the Home, life would have turned out very differently for a lot of us. They could have had a great influence on city government—perhaps on the whole state—because many of the people in politics were graduates of the Home.

It seemed to me that every day at camp was the way Sundays should have been at the Home—loving, joyous, filled with inspiration. But back there, instead of being turned on to Christ, I was beginning to be turned off from religion altogether. I was beginning to be resentful of the strictness and discipline and embittered by the punishment, especially when so much of it seemed undeserved. And Sundays just seemed to be bigger and bigger bores. As far as I was concerned, the only days worse than Sundays were "horror" days and "check" days.

On "check" days, a nurse simply went through the dormitories unannounced and checked everyone for worms. We went to our dorms and stayed there until the nurse came in. Then we pulled down our panties, leaned over the hall tree, and got checked instead of lambasted. If she found anything, we got a spoonful of gaggingly awful medicine and were told to stay close to the bathroom.

But "horror" days were much worse, partly because we were told about them in advance and there was all that time to anticipate the fear and the pain.

"Horror" days were the days we got shots or got vaccinated. We'd be lined up and marched over to the hospital where we'd go through, one at a time, just as though we were in the army. The shots were one quick jab, then were over with, unless your arm swelled up and got real sore, but the vaccinations were the long, slow kind, with lots of little needle pricks like a tatoo. I still have the scar from one, about as big as a half-dollar, on my arm. No one thought about trying to prevent those scars from becoming a disfigurement for life.

But if "horror" days were the worst we had, then holidays were the best days, and we anticipated each one of them with eager excitement for weeks.

For Valentine's Day we were given red and white paper, paste, and crayons and made valentines for the other kids. We could go to the Mart and buy the colored ones that were cut out or the fancy ones that came in their own envelopes, but I made my own so that I could use all my allowance for candy. There were tiny candy hearts with cute sayings on them, and I used to buy a whole sackful and give them to all my favorite friends, especially the boys that I had crushes on. There was a freckle-faced, red-haired boy in fourth grade that I was really "gone" on, and I spent a whole nickel on a valentine for him, but all I got out of it was hurt feelings. When they drew the valentines out of the big cardboard box and passed them out in the schoolroom, the one I got from him was an ugly comic valentine that poked fun at my being fat.

Easter and Christmas were the times we looked forward to the most. For Easter, every kid got a whole new outfit, from the skin out. They gave us a little allowance and took us to the clothing store and let each of us pick out a dress, shoes, hat, and gloves. Then, for fun, we had the Easter-egg hunt. The big kids had the fun of coloring and hiding the eggs, and the little ones had the fun of hunting for them. We'd be lined up, a whistle would be blown, and off we'd go, scrambling around under the trees and bushes to see how many we could find. We were only supposed to get five, but if we found more, we'd give them to someone who didn't have any. There were a few plastic eggs, too, which were colored gold. Each had a slip of paper inside, and whoever found one turned it in for a special prize. I remember one year I found one and got a little pink comb and brush for my prize.

For Lincoln's and Washington's birthdays and other national holidays, we'd read about them in school and make projects such as log cabins. Or we'd act out skits such as Washington's cutting down the cherry tree.

We had plays in the seventh and eighth grades, and I remember rehearsing for weeks and weeks for one. Then came the big day; the play went off like a beautiful dream, and for a couple of days I was a really popular kid.

But the thing that hurt so much was that it was over, all done.

Everything returned to normal. I can remember crying a lot over it. Right from the beginning, I seemed to have that need to act and the craving for attention in my blood.

I guess Halloween was really the most fun, though, because we got to put on funny faces, mess up our hair, put on sheets or anything we could find, and go to the gym for a party.

We could buy little masks at the Mart or we could make our own out of paper sacks or pieces of cloth. One time, in Vacation Bible School, a teacher showed us how to make masks out of papier-mâché. We lined them with cheesecloth and molded them to our faces. Then we painted them to look like the pictures of some African masks that she had in a book, and we made hair out of yarn and string. I was really proud of the one I made, and I saved it in my closet to wear on Halloween.

When I told Claudine about it, she gave me a tan sweater and a bunch of beads and bracelets to wear. She borrowed a grass skirt that a friend of hers had made for a luau and gave me some black stockings to wear with my black shoes. I can remember going to the gym while wearing the mask and thinking that nobody could possibly guess who I was in that costume. But I was wrong!

The first kid I met inside the door said, "Hi, Louise! That's sure a great outfit you've got there," and everybody else knew who I was, too. I could disguise my face, but there was just no way I could disguise my fat body.

We played lots of games and had fun, but I was still disappointed that everyone had recognized me, so when some of the older kids were talking about the mischief they were going to get into after the party, I went along with them.

The teachers, housemothers, and other adults who worked and lived at the Home parked their cars around the edge of the Circle. On the way home from the Halloween parties, it was practically traditional that the kids would let the air out of all the tires. And the boys would get hold of some paint and completely repaint the statue of our founder that stood in the middle of the Circle.

Well, after the party was over and everyone was going back to their dorms, some of us lagged behind and hid in the bushes until everyone had gone past. Then we sneaked up to the cars and started letting the air out of the tires. I was helping when, suddenly one of the men teachers came around the corner of the administration building with a flashlight in his hand. The other kids ducked into the bushes and laid flat on the ground, but I tripped over my too-long grass skirt and landed flat on the concrete.

That's how I learned about tire pumps. I wouldn't squeal on who had helped me do it, so I had to pump up the tires again—all ten of them!

But the boys who had put a shiny coat of gold paint on our founder's statue had a worse job. Becky Albright, who was the worst tattletale in the whole place, saw them doing it and told. They had to clean off all the paint—with toothbrushes!

At Thanksgiving time we always had a tremendous feast. Of course, we had to go to church first and hear about all the blessings for which we were supposed to be grateful. And sometimes, while we were sitting there, the smell of turkey and all the goodies cooking reached us all the way from the kitchen.

There was roast turkey and cranberry sauce and two kinds of potatoes and carrots and peas and dressing and everything you could think of that goes with a Thanksgiving feast. Thanksgiving was one day we could count on that there wouldn't be any cabbage. I hated cabbage, and it seemed that we had more boiled cabbage on weekdays than all the other vegetables put together. There was always pie, and sometimes we even got to have two pieces.

We learned about the Pilgrims and Plymouth Rock in school and we made paper cutouts to decorate the tables: Pilgrims, pumpkins, and turkeys.

But Christmas was the very best time of all. I think we started looking forward to Christmas beginning Thanksgiving night.

We always had a Christmas program in church with special music and sometimes different groups would come out from town and put on a play or cantata for us.

On Christmas Eve we went to the auditorium for the program put on by our own schoolmates. Friends or relatives could come, and after it was over, Santa Claus came with a huge stack of presents, and each one of us got a bundle to carry back to the dorm. When we were older, we got boxes instead, and I was disappointed the first time I got a box, because the boxes were much smaller.

But the bundles were huge, and they were crammed with all kinds of goodies. We'd carry them back to the dorm to unpack them and spread everything out on our beds. Everyone got a doll, games, candy, nuts, fruit, and toys. There was only one thing wrong: they were all the same. Sometimes there would be four or five different kinds of dolls or different toys or games, but every fourth or fifth girl would have one just alike. I know we were very lucky to have had dolls at all, but one time I asked Claudine if she would buy me a doll with a green face just so I could have one that was different from everybody else's.

We had Christmas trees in the dorms and would gather around them in the evening to sing carols. For me, that was the greatest time. There was a group of older kids called the Melodeers who used to come with their ukuleles and sing for us, and I couldn't wait until I got old enough to join them.

But there's one Christmas that stands out from all the rest. It was the saddest and loneliest Christmas I ever spent at the Home. A couple of days before that, Claudine and Granny had come for me on a Saturday, and I had gone to spend the day with them. Claudine wasn't working that day, so she had taken me along to visit a friend of hers who had a niece about my age.

I liked Rosalyn. She wasn't a tomboy like I was, but we got along together real well. She had long, shiny black hair and coal black eyes and the whitest skin I had ever seen. Only today her cheeks were flushed and pink looking.

"Rosalyn isn't feeling very well today," her mother said as we went into the house, "but I'm sure she'll be glad to see Louise."

Well, she *was* glad, and we worked crossword puzzles and played jacks and had a tea party even though she seemed more quiet and listless than usual. Then a few days later, I was quiet and listless too—with a fever of 103!

They put me in a room by myself in the hospital, and two days before Christmas, I broke out with chicken pox. I felt perfectly awful—all itchy and uncomfortable on the outside and dejected and left out on the inside!

I used to envy Rosalyn when I went to her house. She had a father and a mother, a room of her own, and beautiful things she didn't have to share with a single soul. And she used to tell me how lucky I was, because I had the other girls to talk to and play with.

Lying there by myself in the hospital, I came to realize for the first time that maybe I *was* lucky. A little bit, anyway. Because right now I was terribly lonesome, and I missed the other kids dreadfully. The nurses spent all the time with me that they could, but it wasn't the same as being in the middle of all the excitement of Christmas. I couldn't go to the program or the party in the gym, and I was sure I'd miss out on the bundle of presents, too.

Claudine came out on Christmas Eve, and they let her come in and sit with me. She had games, toys, puzzles, and a lot more candy than the nurses would let me eat. She gave me a big, long box all done up in pretty paper and big red bows. I stuck the bows on my nightgown and ripped off the paper. Then I opened the box, and there was the tallest, most beautiful doll I had ever seen. It had long, dark brown hair and big brown eyes that closed, and it said "Mama" when you pressed a certain spot on its back. "She'll walk along with you, too," Claudine said and showed me how. I was ecstatic!

"I'm going to call her Natalie," I said. Natalie Wood was my favorite movie star.

"I brought you a Christmas story, too," Claudine said after a while. "I'll read it to you if you like, because I don't think you're supposed to strain your eyes when you have chicken pox."

One of the nurses brought her a cup of coffee, and she lit up a cigarette even though she wasn't supposed to smoke in the hospital. Then she took this beautiful book out of a bag and started to read, *The Bird's Christmas Carol.*

We got through it—all the way to the end. And when Carol Bird died at the end of the story, we were both sitting there with tears running down our cheeks.

"Oh, darn!" Claudine said softly, "whyinheck didn't they tell me it ended like that? Any blockhead oughtta know that a book called *The Bird's Christmas Carol* should be about birds!"

It was Christmas Eve, and there I was, all by myself, in a room in the hospital. For Claudine, too, it was a miserable ending to a miserable day, but she did her best to do what she could to brighten it.

"Look, honey," she said, wiping her eyes and blowing her nose, "whadda ya say to a couple a hands of gin rummy?" Then she pulled out a deck of cards from her purse and sat there teaching me how to play the game until the nurse came and told her it was time to leave.

4

The Whistle Blew for Me

As long as I could remember, I had been awakened every morning by the four or five short blasts of the whistle that called the kitchen workers to their before-dawn rituals at the Home.

Then one morning the whistle blew for me.

I was in sixth grade, and the time had come for me to start practical training through all the various areas of life at the Home. Kitchen duty was where it all began.

It was still dark when I got up and dressed that morning. It seemed very strange to be the only one in my room who was awake and stirring, and it seemed stranger still to be the only one in the bathroom. *Aha!* I thought. *If you* really *want some privacy around here, the secret is to get up early.*

But when I went downstairs, I met the girls from the floors below who were also on kitchen duty. It didn't seem so bad walking across the campus toward the kitchen with them. Light was breaking in the east, and I stood there entranced by the colors. I had never seen a sunrise before. And the birds—it seemed that a mighty concert was going on, with solos and choruses pouring out of every tree!

Wow! I thought, *If I'd known it was like this, I'd have been up early every morning.*

We went into the kitchen through a back door, and the girls

took some large aprons from their hooks against the wall and gave one to me. They were made out of flour sacks, and I could read the faded printing, but when I put on mine, it hung all the way to the floor. They showed me how to make a big fold across my middle and tie my apron strings in front to hold it up.

We had been in an anteroom, and as we went through the doorway into the kitchen, the first person I saw was Patty's mother.

"Hello, Louise," she greeted me. "It's going to be real nice having you working here with us as part of the team."

I knew she cooked for the staff, but I hadn't realized that she worked in the kitchen, too, and it made me feel warm and secure to find her there. I knew all of the other people by sight, but I didn't feel as close to them as I did to Patty's mother.

I was about to answer her when a movement over her head caught my eye. I looked up and my tongue froze to the roof of my mouth in fear. Over our heads, about a foot below the ceiling, were some large black pipes running the length of the room. And on those pipes were two huge rats, each at least a foot in length. I was terrified at the sight of them and could only stand there trembling.

"Oh, don't mind the rats," Patty's mother laughed. "They're part of the team! They won't bother you unless they're cornered," she tried to comfort me. "They get so much food around here that there's no need for them to take a bite out of people."

But I never did get over my fear of them, not in all the years I was at the Home. There was a broom-and-mop closet at one end of the kitchen which was lit by a single bulb that hung down on its cord from the ceiling. Periodically, the bulb burned out and someone had to go in there, in the dark, to replace the bulb. When it was my turn to do it, I actually held my breath while I unscrewed the burned-out bulb and screwed in the new one for fear a rat would bite me in the dark.

There was also an open freight elevator that was used to bring up supplies from the storage room below into the kitchen. It always seemed to stop about a foot below floor level and every once in a while you'd see these long-nailed toes come over the edge and then the pointed ears and beady eyes of a rat. And sometimes someone would not be looking where he was walking, and forget about that elevator, and fall in.

Once a boy was carrying a sack of flour and when he fell in, it burst open and the flour spilled all over him and all over two big rats. For quite a while, we could pick out those white rats from all the rest.

But that first day in the kitchen was one of the longest days of my life. Patty's mother took me through the kitchen to a room off to one side, and there was the biggest pile of potatoes I had ever seen. She must have noticed the dismayed look on my face because she said softly, "It takes a lot of potatoes to feed all the people we have here."

Even at one potato apiece, it would have taken quite a lot, but by the looks of this pile, they were expecting everyone to eat three or four.

Patty's mother took me over to the sink, got a knife and pan for me, and showed me how to go about it. Five potatoes later, I was ready to quit, but I couldn't even see where we had made a dent in the pile. Two hours later, I could see where we were beginning to make some progress. They hadn't told me before, but now one of the girls broke the news. We had to finish the whole pile before we went to school, even if it meant going without breakfast. I peeled a whole lot faster after that, and by some miracle we got through in time for breakfast.

"Whew!" I said, looking at all those shiny white bodies in their cold-water bath. "That ought to be enough for all week."

"Don't you wish!" one of my fellow peelers replied. "That's only enough for supper."

I had an awful time trying to write in school that day. There was a whopping big blister between my thumb and first finger, and my whole hand ached from my labors. But next morning, I was right back there again, facing another pile of potatoes—and the next morning, and the next, and the next.

But I learned how to peel potatoes, and I guess the reason why we have mostly baked potatoes at my house is because they don't have to be peeled, just scrubbed with a brush.

I learned a lot of other things while I was sitting there keeping my hands busy and my eyes and ears open. I learned about weevils for one thing. They are tiny, hard brown bugs that got into the flour. So the flour was just sifted and used anyway. Or sometimes the weevils would be baked into cookies right along with the nuts and raisins. At least, that way, we didn't have a protein-deficiency problem.

I learned about bread pudding, too. They took the bread the rats had chewed on and tore off the chewed places and made pudding or stuffing out of it or added it to the hamburgers.

The first time we had bread pudding for dessert after that—and I knew I had to eat it or be punished—I almost threw up right there at the table.

Next morning, I told Patty's mother about it when in the kitchen where I was helping her fix some vegetables for salad. "I know how you feel, honey," she said. "It makes me sick to my stomach too, but there's one thing that helps a little. The heat from the cooking or baking kills any germs, so there's really nothing in there that can hurt you. And besides, when we go to a restaurant, we don't really know what might be in the things they serve us, either."

Then one morning I was liberated from the potato-peeling squad and transferred to the pot-washing detail. I've often wished I had a picture of some of the things that went on there.

There were huge iron pots on cranes that swung out from the stove. They were loaded with vegetables or soup for cooking and then swung back over the heat. When they were empty, we had to wash them.

We climbed up on little wooden ladders and took a mop with a long wooden handle and mopped the inside of the pots. There was a drain plug at the bottom of each pot, and we had to pull it out to drain and rinse the pot. Sometimes it was quite a trick to get the plugs out, so to make it easier, we took hold of the edge of the pot, did a forward somersault and landed on our feet inside.

But working the dishwashers was the most fun. We loaded these huge racks with dishes, and they'd run along on a continuous belt, through the dishwater and then through the rinse water.

We could control the temperature of the water so, on hot summer days, we'd cool it way down and ride right along through the rinse water with the dishes. Most of the time, we only did that on Saturdays because that was the day we had to clean everything thoroughly, and we had lots more time to fool around in there without any adults being around.

I still have a scar to remind me of those times because, one day I was sudsing the glasses before stacking them upside down in the dishwasher, and I was laughing so hard at Patty with water streaming off her hair and nose as she rode through the rinse water, that I didn't notice that one of the glasses was chipped. Suddenly I felt this pain across my finger and when I looked down, blood was dripping into the dishwater. Well, I learned that lesson! I've never put my hand into a glass to wash it that way again.

Sometimes on Saturdays we'd take a portable radio with us and practice jitterbugging while we were cleaning up the kitchen. We'd go in the corner by the mop closet and go through all the gyrations. When any of the boys came over, we'd squeal, run, and act silly. But, big as I am, I've always been very light on my feet, and I learned how to do all the steps in a hurry.

We learned by experience everything that had to be done around the Home. There were floor-scrubbing details, room-cleaning details, bathroom-cleaning details, and then there was the laundry.

Every morning before school and every afternoon after school we were given a big bundle of clothes to iron, and we had to finish every last piece of it before we could leave the ironing boards.

On Mondays and Tuesdays, we ironed the little kids' clothes. On Wednesdays and Thursdays we ironed the older kids' clothes, and on Fridays and Saturdays we ironed the linens: napkins, tablecloths, and pillow cases. The things we hated most were little girls' dresses. I had blisters on every finger, it seemed, from trying to poke the pointed end of the iron into all those ruffles and lace-trimmed collars.

Then, just about the time we were getting tall enough to reach the ironing board without having to stand on a box, we were put on the mangle and taught how to iron sheets. To this day, I can't fold a sheet very well by myself, but I'm a real whiz at it if someone grabs the other end.

One autumn evening I had finished my chores and my homework early, so I went outside and climbed up my favorite tree. No one was around, so I was hanging from a branch by my knees, just hanging there thinking. My eye was caught by what looked like a wad of spider webs tucked up under a lower branch, close to the trunk of the tree.

I swung down to the ground and picked up a stick and was just going to poke at it when I heard someone behind me. It was Patty's mother. I hadn't seen her come around the corner of the building.

"If you poke at it, Louise, you'll injure it," she said. "Then it won't turn into a butterfly."

"But that's what you told me about the worm," I reminded her. "Do you mean this fuzzy thing is a butterfly, too?"

"Yes," she said. "It could even be the same one. You see, after the caterpillar has grown as much as it can, it climbs into a protected place like that, fastens itself to a branch, and goes to sleep. Then a change called 'metamorphosis' takes place, and when it comes out of that little brown bag, it has turned into a butterfly."

"You mean that first the butterfly was inside the caterpillar, and now it's inside this thing?" I asked her.

"Not exactly," she said. "First, the thing that is going to become a butterfly *was* a caterpillar. Now it is a pupa. And when it emerges from that little sack, it will be a butterfly. You can't *see* the butterfly inside the caterpillar, even if you cut it open. It's there as a spark of life, an idea that can only be seen when it *becomes* what it was intended to be."

I waited until she had disappeared around the corner of her own building, then I picked up the stick again and knocked the little brown thing off the tree. I poked it open, expecting to see some kind of spark flare up for an instant, but nothing happened. Then I crouched down on the ground and looked more closely and what I saw, made me draw back in horror, for there, unmistakably, was the delicate trace of tiny, folded wings.

A mingled feeling of grief and fear swept over me—remorse, guilt, and then panic. Grabbing up the murdered butterfly in my fist, I took off after Patty's mother as fast as I could run. But as I rounded the corner of her building, I saw that I was too late. She was inside already, and it was after hours, so I wasn't allowed to follow her.

Confused, bewildered, and heartsick, I looked at the tiny chrysalis turned coffin. Then very gently, I poked it deep down inside the petals of a big, yellow chrysanthemum and walked slowly back to my dorm.

As I reached the building, Patty met me with a mop in her hand. She was on her way to stand it in the drying rack outside the door. "Guess who lucked out on mop detail," she grumbled. Then, "Oh, yeah. Your grandmother called. She said to tell you your mother's home."

5

What I Thought I Didn't Have

I had no memory of my father, and because my mother was ill so much of the time when I was little, we had never had an opportunity to develop a real close mother-daughter relationship.

I was fond of her and was always glad to see her, but I had no feeling of dependency upon her and, consequently, felt no deep sense of loss when she was away.

In the unquestioning way of children, I had accepted her illness and the fact that she could not take care of me. Her gradual recovery had not effected any changes in my personal life, and I suppose it was because of this that I could also accept the news of her second marriage in the same detached, unemotional way.

One Saturday while I was at Granny's, my mother came in with this tall stranger in an army uniform. I was told that they were going to be married and that they would be going away to live in France. I shook hands with the stranger, accepted the news without comment, and asked Claudine if I could have a peanut-butter-and-jelly sandwich. Then I went out in the backyard and played with the dog.

Through the years after that, there had been many picture postcards and, occasionally, a music box, a cuddly toy animal, and sometimes a lovely French doll. I loved those presents, but the greatest satisfaction I got from them was not in playing with them, but in taking them back to the Home and flaunting them in front of Cory and the other stuck-up girls.

"Look what my mother sent me from France," I'd brag, parading my new toy up and down the dorm. It was my way of getting even for the hurts—real and imagined—that they had inflicted upon me.

Although it was called an orphan's home, there were only a few real orphans there. For most of us, like myself, it was actually a boarding school and our relatives paid to keep us there. Naturally, there were inequities. Some of the girls, like Cory, were "rich kids." And some, like Patty, were "poor kids." The rest of us, I guess, were just middle class.

Although Claudine saw to it that I never wanted a thing, I still envied the girls like Cory. Probably not so much for what they had as for the fact that they were popular.

Cory had lived in places such as Los Angeles and New York. She had flown in an airplane and had been to the theater and had gone sailing at Cape Cod. She could talk for hours about the things she had done and the places she had seen, and I yearned for just one of those experiences. The girls flocked around her in the dorm and the boys hung around her at school, and I was jealous of that, too.

And so, to make up for what I thought I didn't have, I started fantasizing. I had always longed for a home and a mother and father, a room of my own and a sister and brother of my own. I envied Patty because her mother was there working at the Home and because she had a sister and two brothers who were there, too. But that was the *only* home they had, and Patty envied me because I could go to my Granny's on Saturdays.

As I grew older, the elegant home I was going to have "someday" began to take on shape and form. I pictured spacious lawns, with trees and flowerbeds, and a swimming pool. And I began to furnish the house with lavishly decorated rooms from pictures in magazines, on television, and in catalogs. The dreaming was harmless enough in itself—until it started to take on substance from the lovely presents that arrived from France.

Instead of projecting my dream onto an always out-of-reach "someday," I began making up little lies about what we were going to do and where we were going to live when my mother and my new stepfather came back from France. And somewhere in all of the spinning, I got caught in the web myself, until I actually believed it.

When Patty told me about the phone call, suddenly the whole dream seemed true. They were here! They were coming for me! They were going to take me out of this place, and we'd move into a beautiful home, and I'd have a room of my own at last! I lay awake on my bed for a long time that night, much too excited to sleep. Then, suddenly, it was morning. The 5:30 whistles were blowing, and I bounced out of bed even though it was Saturday, and I didn't need to get up because I was no longer on kitchen duty.

For once in my life, I scarcely noticed the food I was served at breakfast. "My mother's coming for me today," I told Patty, as soon as grace had been said and everyone started talking. "Will you help me pack my clothes?"

"Gee, I'd like to," she said, "but I have mop detail, remember?"

So right after breakfast, I hurried back to the dorm and started hauling things out of my closet. I decided to keep the pictures of Andy Williams and Natalie Wood, but a lot of my souvenirs and keepsakes went into a cardboard box for the other girls to have. I folded my clothes and put them in other boxes, and every few minutes, I'd run to the window to see if Granny's car had arrived.

Somehow the morning wore on. And pretty soon it was time to go to Manna Hall for lunch. This time I hardly ate anything at all. I couldn't imagine what was keeping them, and a funny, sickish feeling centered in my stomach.

Then, on the way back from Manna Hall, I saw them. My mother and the man she had married were walking on the sidewalk outside the gate, and he was carrying a child in his arm. No one had told me they had a baby! But she was wearing a dress, and she had white stockings and black shoes. Oh, good! I had a baby sister at last. I realized that they were walking around out there, waiting for the welcome center to open. I ran around the corner of the building and looked in the parking area for Granny's car, but it wasn't there. The sickish feeling clutched at my stomach once more.

Slowly, I started toward the gate and saw them coming toward me. Then I realized my stepfather wasn't carrying a child at all. It was an enormous doll, with curly blond hair, and I knew they had brought it for me. A wonderful feeling of relief came over me, and I ran the rest of the way to meet them.

After the greetings were over, "I'll get my clothes," I said, and started for the dorm.

"Oh, uh, not just yet, Louise," my mother called after me, and the sickish feeling came back again.

I was glad we didn't go into the welcome center. Instead, we walked over to a clump of trees and sat down on the grass in the shade. They were only going to be here for a little while, my mother told me. Then they were going to visit some of our relatives in Arkansas, and after that, they'd be going back to France again.

I should have realized that my stepfather was a career man in the army and that they would always be moving around from one place to another, but I had let the fantasy get out of control. Gradually the truth filtered through my aching disappointment, and I came back to hard reality. There probably would never be a big, beautiful home with a room in it just for me. If I wanted things like that, I'd have to pitch in and work for them myself.

I waited until everyone else had gone out of the dorm. Then I went in and unpacked my clothes and all the rest of the day I tried to think up something to tell the other girls.

I was glad it was my day to work in the Mart because I wouldn't have to talk to anyone until I had the whole thing thought out and I'd had a chance to get over the hurt a little.

Work details were divided up so that everyone had a chance to work on everything that had to be done. That way, the duties were shared equally and each one of us had a chance to learn how to do all the different chores.

I liked working in the Mart best of all. It was a kind of general store right there on campus—a combination sweet shop and dime store. There were school supplies, hair ribbons, a large assortment of candy, and an ice-cream counter. Two or three of us worked in there at the same time, but I always volunteered to dish up the ice-cream cones, because ice cream and I had a love affair going.

Whenever you got down to the bottom of one of those big five-gallon cartons, there was always a generous "sample" stuck to the sides and bottom. When I got through with them, those cartons were *clean!* On this particular day, I didn't wait to reach bottom on one of the cartons. I just went in there and buried my disappointment in ice cream—five or six different kinds!

And all the while I was sacking candy and scooping up ice cream, I tried to think up some story about why I hadn't gone off with my parents. The plots of several movies came to mind, but none of them seemed to work. Maybe it was because most of them were tangled up in cowboys and horses.

I had tried everything I could think of by the time I was ready to leave the Mart, and on my way back to the dorm, I came to the conclusion that there wasn't anything that would work except just telling the truth. But, right after supper we went to the auditorium for the movie. This time it was *The Wizard of Oz* which is a longer picture than we usually had. By the time we got back to the dorm, we had barely enough time to get ready for bed before the bell would ring for "lights out."

Patty and I were ready for bed and were sitting on the edge of my bed, talking about my new doll when Patty realized that Cory was missing.

Cory was such a small-boned, petite little thing that she seemed younger than we were, but she was actually two years older and quite mature for her age. Her mother was on the stage, and Cory had moved around so much that she was behind in her schoolwork which put her in our grade in school instead of being with the girls her own age.

But what Cory lacked in academic knowledge, she made up for in other ways. Cory had been around. She was developing and filling out her sweaters a lot faster than the rest of us in our room. And Cory knew how to get along with boys. There was this one boy in school who she had quite a crush on, and the two of them were always thinking up ways to sneak off to be together. Sometimes they'd meet at the Circle on Sundays where only the brothers and sisters were supposed to meet. And once they were caught kissing under the bleachers at a football game. Well, we didn't know it then, but that night they had decided to sneak away after the movie and stay out all night.

Besides Patty, Cory, and me, there were two other girls in our room: Elvira Ellington, the bookworm and straight-A student; and Becky Albright, the stool pigeon. We were lucky because Becky was with her mother on an overnight pass and wouldn't be back until morning.

"Golly," I groaned when I realized Cory wasn't back yet and bed check would be coming up in a few minutes. "Patty, what are we going to do?" I was jealous of Cory's popularity with the others, but I didn't want to see her punished.

Suddenly Patty jerked up straight and grabbed my new doll. "I've got an idea!" she said. "Can I borrow this for a little while?"

"Sure," I told her. "What're you going to do?"

"Watch," she said, hurrying over to Cory's bed. She stuffed my doll under the covers, wadded up a towel and a pillow to make up for what the doll lacked in size, and arranged the sheet with just enough blond hair showing to pass for Cory's yellow curls. Elvira watched without comment. In spite of the fact that she was such a square, she was really a good egg, too, and we knew she'd never tell. Then we scuttled under our own covers just as the housemother came into the room and flashed her light around to make sure everyone was in bed.

"But how will she get in when she comes back?" I asked, sitting up in bed after I was sure the housemother was gone.

"I don't know," Patty whispered. "I wish we could think of something to help her."

"Why don't we leave the window open and put a chair down there on this side of the bushes," Elvira said. "That way, she can climb in and pull in the chair after her."

It was a terrific idea, and it worked! About two o'clock in the morning, I heard a rustling outside the window. Cory had come back and was going to try to rap on the window to awaken us. Then she found the chair and did just as Elvira had said. She climbed through the window, pulled in the chair after her, and I saw that she was soaking wet.

She and her boyfriend had decided to spend the night under the trees down by the bulrush pond, but they forgot about the night watchman. When they saw his car coming around and his spotlight shining over the grounds, they ran toward the pond to hide in the rushes and both of them fell in.

But the next time Cory went off campus, she brought each of us a pound box of Fanny Farmer's chocolates, and we were the best of friends from then on.

The excitement over Cory's close call helped to alleviate my disillusionment about going to live with my mother, but not for long. By breakfast time next morning, I was feeling the hurt all over again. And because I hurt so much, I tried to cover it with an I-don't-care attitude, but Patty's mother saw through the facade.

"Why don't you come over with the children after dinner?" she asked. "We're going to make some fudge."

It was Sunday, and they were all going to meet in her rooms instead of getting together out at the Circle with the rest of the boys and girls, so I went along with Patty right from Manna Hall.

We didn't have too long a time, but we made divinity fudge, my favorite. That's the kind you make with egg whites and lots of nuts. The boys cracked and shelled the nuts, Patty and her little sister got everything ready, and Patty's mother and I beat the egg whites. We did have fun, and I even got to take a little bagful of fudge back to the dorm with me.

Patty had to leave early, because it was her turn to mop the hall, and I must have dawdled too long because the bell rang for rest time just as I was going up the stairs. I stuffed the candy into a drawer in my closet, grabbed a book off the shelf, and scooted for my bed.

I had just taken off my shoes and stretched out when Patty

came in—late. "I tripped over the darn pail and spilled water all over the floor just after I finished mopping it up," she muttered as she passed my bed.

We weren't supposed to talk at rest time. We weren't even supposed to whisper. We were supposed to be absolutely quiet. So Becky Albright got up from her bed and went and told on Patty.

With any other housemother, Patty probably would have gotten away with it, in view of her accident with the mop pail, but our regular housemother was away this Sunday, and her substitute was Mrs. Ridgeley. I shivered for Patty in anticipation of what was coming.

Sure enough! In a moment, Becky was back with Mrs. Ridgeley right behind her. And in her hand was one of those long linoleum strips. She marched over to Patty's bed, grabbed her by an ear, and almost dragged her out into the hall. From my bed, I could see Patty's legs as she bent over the hall tree. We could all hear the thwack! thwack! as the linoleum hit her, but I could see the red stripes on her legs.

Patty didn't make a sound, but when it was over and Mrs. Ridgeley had left, she went into the bathroom and put cold water on her legs before she came back to our room. As she came through the door, she saw Becky smirking at her, and with her lips, she framed the words, "I hate your guts!"

Patty hadn't made a sound. She hadn't even whispered, but Becky bounced out of bed again and went straight to Mrs. Ridgeley. This time, she came back with a wooden paddle. Patty's legs were still red from the whipping as she bent over the hall tree again.

I couldn't bear to look so I shoved my face into my pillow, but I could still hear the smack of that paddle on Patty's bare flesh. I knew Patty was gritting her teeth. I knew she wouldn't cry out if it killed her so, when I heard a moan from her, I turned around and looked.

I knew I could get a thrashing too, if I got out of that bed, but when I saw the blood running down Patty's legs, I bolted. Down the stairs and straight for the dean's office—in my stocking feet.

Mrs. Emerson, the dean of women, was the one for whom I sometimes baked pecan pies. When I blurted out that Patty was bleeding, she called one of the directors and the two of them hurried back to the dorm with me. I had never seen Mrs. Emerson angry before, but when she saw Patty—and Mrs. Ridgeley still standing there with the paddle in her hand—her face turned as white as her hair.

Patty was standing there, too, with clenched fists and clenched teeth. There was blood on the hall tree, the floor, the paddle, and blood running down Patty's legs onto her bobby socks.

They took Patty to the hospital, and later I learned that before they fired her, they made Mrs. Ridgeley go to the hospital and apologize to Patty. We never saw her again, but that didn't do a thing to help Patty's suffering or to ease her mother's anguish. The worry over her children, the silent suffering she went through when they were abused, finally proved too much for her. Before Patty got out of the hospital, her mother had been taken to another one, with complete nervous exhaustion.

A few days after the incident with Patty, I was hurrying down the hall ahead of Becky Albright as we were on the way to breakfast. At the head of the stairs, I bent over suddenly to tie my shoe. Becky went hurtling over me and tumbled all the way to the bottom. When the report came back to us from the hospital that she had sprained her wrist, I wished she had broken her neck!

But we got rid of Becky anyway. When she came back from the hospital, we put her in Coventry. That meant that none of the girls in our dorm would talk to her. We acted like she wasn't even there. Then, as the story got around campus about how she had tattled on Patty, other kids started ignoring her, too.

After three weeks of that, she had all she could take. One day her mother came and got her and that was the last we saw of Becky. We learned later that she was going to public school.

6

Myclaudine

I felt lost without Patty. We had been best friends ever since fourth grade when she first came to the home. Her father was disabled and was in and out of veterans' hospitals most of the time. Faced with four little children to support, and having no particular job skills, Patty's mother had brought them to the Home and was working there to help pay for their board and room.

While she was in the hospital, I went to see Patty every day and took her little presents I bought at the Mart—such as comic books and a little toy dog that danced in a circle and wagged his tail when you wound him up.

It hurt me to see her lying there face down, waiting for her legs and bottom to heal so she could sit in a chair again. But the nurses were so good to her! They propped a pillow under her chest so she could watch television, and they came in and talked with her every chance they got.

Granny and Claudine came to get me the following Saturday, and as we were driving home, I told them all about the things that had happened to Patty. Well! Claudine was all for turning around right in the middle of the street and going back to the Home for my things. She wasn't about to leave me in a place where they beat poor defenseless little kids!

They argued about it for a few more blocks, and Granny finally cooled her down. "They fired Mrs. Ridgeley," Granny told her, "and no teacher in her right mind is going to lay a hand on one of those kids now and take a chance on losing her job."

Finally Claudine agreed to drive on home. "You let me know if one of those harpies so much as lays a hand on you, ya hear?" she told me almost fiercely.

"Okay," I promised, feeling secure and protected again in her implied threats to anyone who would dare to harm me. Claudine had always been the dominant person in my life. Before I was born, she had told all her friends that she didn't want to be a grandmother, but after I arrived on the scene, she took over completely.

It was Claudine who came to the hospital and got me when my mother had to stay there, and it was Claudine who bathed and fed and dressed me, who got up for the two o'clock feedings and walked the floor with me when I had colic. She was aggressively defensive of me; she spoiled me; she saw to it that I never wanted for a thing; and she was the one person I could always count on no matter what happened in my life.

Whenever there was anything going on at the Home that parents or relatives could come to, Claudine was there. And even though I might have spent all day Saturday with her, she'd drive out again to be with me on Sunday during visiting time. On holidays and my birthday she was there, too, with bags and boxes of goodies and all kinds of presents.

For Easter, we were always taken to the clothing store over the Mart to pick out a whole new Easter outfit: dress, shoes, hat, and white gloves. Then Claudine would come out and bring me another complete outfit. Sometimes I even had three frilly new dresses, ruffled petticoats, and straw hats with flowers.

At Christmas there were always lots of presents under the tree at Granny's house, but Claudine would come out to the Home just the same and bring me pretty boxes of talcum powder and perfumed soap, a white chenille bathrobe with slippers to match, and knitted hat, scarf, and mitten sets.

If there was any excuse at all for coming out to the Home, Claudine would be there.

When I was little and the other kids picked on me, or when I was just mad at them, I'd always say, "I'll tell my Claudine on you," and everyone in my dorm thought her name was Myclaudine, because that's what I always called her, "My Claudine."

I knew she had married very young, but the marriage was not successful. I knew my grandfather and thought he was great. Sometimes he'd come to the Home to get me on Saturdays in his old green truck, but he always let me off in front of the house and never came in. "Your grandfather's a good enough sort," she used to tell me by way of explanation as I got older, "but we just don't get along. When we get together it's like flint and tinder." Like the fact of my mother's illness, this was something I accepted without asking why.

One summer, a friend of hers had asked Claudine to help her out with her housekeeping duties at a large motel. After a few months of learning the business firsthand—and with the prodding of her friend—she had applied for a housekeeping job on her own. By the time I went to the Home, she was executive housekeeper for one of the largest hotels in our city.

Outwardly, she often seemed harsh and cantankerous, but her heart was a glob of goo, especially when little kids or people down on their luck were concerned. Right now, her attention focused on Patty and "those other poor little kids." Without their mother—and with their dad in the hospital, too—they were really in a spot by Claudine's estimation. So, as soon as Patty was able to get around again, she and one of the other kids in her family went home with me each Saturday. And when we went back, we always took little "care packages" to give out to the others when we met them at the Circle on Sundays. I wasn't supposed to be there because they weren't my brothers or sisters, but I never got into trouble for taking those goodies to them from Claudine. That fall, we were going into high school, and there was a real thrill when the seniors moved out in June, and we moved into the last building we would occupy on campus.

But other changes were taking place also, and those little white cotton undershirts just weren't doing it for us anymore.

The holes in Patty's panties had been a source of embarrassment to her for a couple of weeks, but with her mother gone, she didn't know what to do about it. Whenever she washed them in the bathroom at night, she was washing her slip also and covering them with that. She could have asked Claudine to loan her some money for new ones, but Patty hadn't been raised to ask anyone for help.

Then on Saturday, when she was working in the clothing store above the Mart, she thought she found an answer. Cautiously, she slid a package of panties and a couple of bras over on the counter and then onto the floor. When she was locking up that night, she picked up the packages and hid them under her skirt, but the night watchman had seen her and stopped her outside the door.

Red faced and embarrassed to tears, she showed him what was in the packages. "I really need them desperately, Mr. Coleman," she explained, and told him about the holes. He probably realized that she needed the bras pretty desperately, too, and I'm sure he understood what an effort it was for her to tell him.

"There, there, honey," he consoled her, because the tears were coming pretty fast by then. "No young lady should ever have to steal things like that." He opened his wallet and gave her enough money to pay for them. Then he drew out another five-dollar bill and gave her that, too. "I want you to be sure those brothers of yours aren't going around with holes in their socks either," he said. "If any of you kids need anything like that again, I want you to come to me."

In a couple of months, one of those changes caught up with me, too. I woke up one morning to find blood on the sheet and blood on my pajamas. When I went into the bathroom, I was sure there must be something terribly wrong inside of me even though I didn't have any pain.

I was standing there panic stricken, wondering what I should do, when Elvira walked in. She filled me in on all the details I had missed when the public health nurse had shown us that "growing up" film in the auditorium.

I learned to accept "the curse" as another fact of life, and the only time it really gave me any trouble was when it interfered with my swimming.

We girls went over to the gym on designated days of the week to use the same equipment and go out for all the sports that the boys did. We had baseball, volleyball, basketball, tennis, track, and all the rest. We worked out on the athletic equipment, did shot puts, high jumps, and all those Olympic-type things, and we had water sports and swimming.

The ball games were all right, and I could usually be counted on to make my share of points for my team, but I detested track. I was too fat to care all that much about running, and the hurdles were too much! So, whenever I had to get out there and go chasing around that track, I'd have a convenient attack of asthma, and I'd be allowed to sit on the bench.

But I loved swimming, and that's where I excelled. I could lie on my back in the water with my legs crossed and my hands under my head and float around that way for hours. I did fairly well with the crawl and the breaststroke, too, but nobody could beat me at the backstroke. Nobody. Not even the boys. I'd get in that water and start churning across that pool with my arms flying around like propellers on a ship, and nobody could get anywhere near me for speed.

There was this team called the Frogmen, and if you were good enough to get on it and could pass the tests, you got a lifesaving and lifeguard badge you could wear on your swimming suit. I was always trying to do something to keep up with the other kids since I was so heavy, so I decided to try out for Frogmen. The first thing we had to do was stay in the water for forty-five minutes without getting out or touching the sides of the pool. For me that was duck soup! They didn't tell you how you had to stay in there so, while the other kids were treading water or tiring themselves out just swimming around, I flipped over on my back and floated. There was this big two-hundred-pound dummy that was dressed in blue jeans and a cap. It would be thrown in the pool and when it hit the water, we had to dive in and "rescue" it. Whenever it was my turn to rescue "Herman," I'd come up from beside it like a broaching whale and get a neck hold on it. Then I'd roll over on my back and tow it to the side of the pool. I could do it so fast and so easily that one day one of the boys challenged me. He was a long, lean blond kid who was always needling me anyway.

"Yeah," he sneered when I got my second medal, "you think you're pretty good, don't cha. Well, I'll bet you couldn't pull a drowning person out if he was alive and kicking!"

"You don't think so, huh," I retorted. Then with one quick flip of my arm, I knocked him into the pool and dived in after him. Before he could surface, I grabbed him by a handful of shaggy blond hair and towed him three times around the pool, kicking, spluttering, and trying his best to get loose. Every time he reached up to pull my hand away, I shoved his face back under the water and after that, no one ever challenged me again.

By the time we left the Home, we had been given enough vocational training to qualify us for jobs in several different kinds of work, so that in addition to housekeeping chores, we also learned varityping and press work in the print shop, filing and clerical work in the radio studio there on the grounds, hospital work, and cosmetology.

That's where I ran into another one of those paradoxes that was always cropping up around the Home. By that time, we had another one of those screaming, shouting, Bible-slapping, foot-stomping preachers, and this one turned me off from religion entirely.

"Don't you associate with no Mexicans," he would say, shaking his finger at all those rows and rows of kids. "Don't you talk to no niggers. Don't you let the devil git holt of you through smokin' and drinkin'." That was for all of us, but he had a special admonition just for the girls. "Don't you go primpin' yourselves up," he'd shout. "Don't you go paintin' your faces like street-walkers and whores!"

So here we were in cosmetology class, and they were teaching us how to apply makeup and color our hair! But any trepidation I might have had about that had disappeared along with my respect for preachers and acceptance of their preaching. Because I disliked the man and his manners so thoroughly, I had less and less faith in his message.

I used all the cosmetics I could get my hands on, and I colored my hair a different color almost every week. From its natural nothing-blond color, I went to ash blond, golden blond, platinum blond and then back down the color scale again from brownette to red, auburn, and finally black.

And the boys were beginning to pay more attention to me too. At first, they'd only let us sit together when we went to the movies, but this boy Jimmy and I used to make eyes at one another and exchange notes and linger in the halls after school. Once we got together under the bleachers at a football game, and when we saw one of the teachers coming, we pretended he was helping me to find my ring. I took off the pretty little agate ring Claudine had bought me and dropped it in the dirt, but when the teacher came to see what we were doing, he accidentally stepped on it and broke it.

And they would let us sit together in church so we'd go over there and sit as far back as we could and hold hands during the sermon. And right after Manna Hall and Sunday dinner, we'd go over to the Circle where the brothers and sisters met and would fool around there until somebody spotted us and sent us back to our dorms.

By this time the incongruities between the preaching and the practice were becoming more and more apparent to me, and I was starting to feel rebellious and embittered toward the Home.

The realization that I would probably never live with my mother made me feel resentful toward having to stay there, and Patty's situation made me feel bitter about some of the staff. In place of the stoical attitude and placid acceptance of things I had had for so long, I was beginning to chafe at the rules and to think of religion as a scare tactic for frightening the devil out of little kids to keep them in line.

In my feelings and conversation, the Home had always been "our" and "we." Now it was beginning to change to "we" and "they." "We" had to do what "they" told us to. "They" were exploiting us by making us do all their dirty work.

Then something happened to reinforce those attitudes and start my life on a horribly destructive detour.

7

The Girls Called "Fast"

I don't know what the reasons were for doing it—whether the Home became too crowded or the academic requirements changed—but in our sophomore year, we began being bused outside the Home to high school.

This was a very large new school with an enrollment of 2800 or more, and when we first rolled up there in that old blue bus with the name of the Home painted across it, we were scared and embarrassed half to death.

We filed off that bus one by one and there stood all those kids laughing at us. "Whooo-ee! Look at the orphans! Hi, Orphan Annie! What is that Home you go to, anyway? Some kind of a church?"

We had a dress code out at the Home. The boys all had neat haircuts and they only wore blue jeans when they were doing their chores. The girls wore bobby socks and oxfords and skirts and sweaters, but the sweaters had to be bulky and the skirts had to come to just below the knee.

Well! I couldn't believe the way these kids were dressed. Just any old thing seemed to go, and I felt like blushing when I saw how tight those girls' sweaters were. And when I actually saw that some of the boys inside that fence were smoking! Well, I couldn't believe my eyes.

But we got used to it, and after a while, we managed to fit

ourselves into the scene just as if we had always gone there. The girls at high school wore culottes which we weren't allowed to wear at the Home. So we saved our allowances and went over to the shopping center across from the school and bought culottes. We'd wear our skirts over them while on the bus, then go to the bathroom and take off our skirts when we got to school.

I had been at the Home for so many years and had been so protected, that I really didn't know what the world was like outside the Home. Now I found that the things that preacher had tried to pound into us just didn't seem to make much sense.

"Don't you associate with no Catholics!" he used to yell. "Don't you wear short skirts and make a dis-play of your limbs!" Well, at school, the only girls who didn't wear short skirts or culottes were the ones who came from the Home. We couldn't do anything about the length of our skirts so we saved our money and bought culottes so we wouldn't feel so old-fashioned and be so conspicuous in the crowd.

There were so many adjustments to make all at once! Just finding our way around the different classrooms was enough of a chore without trying to fit in socially. And trying to catch up in our classwork was another scary job. They had given us a good education at the Home, but we weren't prepared for subjects such as geometry, calculus, and biology.

But after a while, we settled in with the rest and began to be accepted. We got in with some of the cliques and joined the different groups and clubs and so on.

At the Home, I had finally gotten in with the Melodeers and had learned to play the ukulele. We entertained the rest of the kids and put on skits now and then, so when tryouts were announced for the Thespians, the school drama group, I tried out and got a part.

I joined the athletic team, too, and every other group I could get into. So much of the time at the Home I had felt so lonely and left out. Now I tried to make up for it by getting in with all the kids I could and doing anything to attract attention.

Every time there was casting for the school operettas, I'd try out for those too, but most of the time the girls who had taken vocal lessons got the parts.

I did get the part of Hattie, the maid, in *Kiss Me Kate,* though, and along with a pretty good speaking part, I also got to sing "Another Opening." I wasn't good, but I was loud, and this time it helped. I could project my voice all the way to the back of the auditorium without a mike, while the girl I was up against had taken lessons and had a good voice but during tryouts she got stage fright and her voice came out in a thin little murmur. Except for one time, I was never the least bit timid about going before an audience.

Those operettas really opened our eyes. Except for that part as Hattie, I was in the chorus along with Patty, and we had to go in after supper several evenings a week for operetta practice.

By that time we were allowed to have dates with boys at the Home, but they were on campus. We could walk over to the Mart together to buy ice cream; we could go to sports events together, and we'd be allowed to sit together at the movies or in church. But now some of the boys from high school wanted to take us out which was a whole different picture.

First of all, the boy had to come out to the Home, and sometimes his parents had to come with him. He was asked everything, almost as if he were going into the army. The poor kids would get so embarrassed that many didn't come back. If a guy did stick it out and we went out, it had to be on a Friday night and we had to be back by 11:00 P.M. He could come back on Saturday night and go to the movies on campus, but we couldn't leave the grounds two nights in a row. He could come back again Sunday night, too, if he wanted to, but we had to go to church if he did.

All that red tape didn't set very well with those boys from high school, so we didn't have many dates at first, but then Patty and I began to observe that the girls who were most popular with the boys were the ones we called "fast." They wore lipstick and they made up their eyes. They used slangy expressions, some of which were cusswords to us, and they smoked cigarettes!

So we went to the shopping center across from school and got cigarettes from the vending machines, because the machines didn't ask how old you were—all you needed was money. Then we'd take them back to the Home in our lunch pails or hide them in our pockets and slip them into our shoe boxes or some other hiding place in our closets.

There was a bathroom between every two bedrooms in the older girls' dorm, so we'd go into the bathroom and lock both doors, then we'd sit in the window to smoke so the smoke wouldn't go into the room. We'd puff and blow, puff and blow, noisily and showily, and once in a while a trace would get into our lungs and set up a regular coughing fit.

Neither Patty nor I ever did inhale, but Cory did and got hooked on them. When Elvira saw what we were up to, she just shook her head like we were a couple of two-year-olds, but she didn't ever tell on us.

The people at the Home regarded dancing as a sin, so they never let us go to the school dances, but they did let us go off campus for operetta rehearsals. Well, we dreamed up more operetta rehearsals than it would have taken to put on three or four operettas. At first they called the school to see if we were really there, but after two or three times, I guess it got embarrassing, so they didn't call anymore. That's when we started using rehearsals as an excuse when we dated the high-school boys.

We always had to go out in our operetta costumes, but we'd sneak a sweater and culottes underneath them and change in a filling station, because I had torn my costume one night, and the housemothers were all shook up when they had to make me a new one.

We had to be in by eleven-o'clock curfew. The cars would line the street and the hugging and kissing would go on until one minute of eleven. Or sometimes the couples would lean against the wall, all twined up in each other's arms. It wasn't so much a case of being madly in love as it was a case of riling Harding. She was the housemother who had to stand by the gate and lock it at eleven.

She'd yell, "Stop that! Stop it, I say," at one couple and get them untangled while another couple would go to smooching and hugging like mad.

But that game got old after a while, so Patty and I decided to run the risk of being "campused" by trying a scheme for staying out later.

My Granny had been right when she said no housemother would ever whip a kid at the Home again after they fired Ridgeley for beating Patty. Instead of beatings, they thought up a cold-war kind of punishment which was called "campusing." For punishment we had to stay on campus. We couldn't go to the movies or any other activity except school and church, and we weren't allowed to have visitors.

We knew that if we were caught in what we were going to do, we'd probably be campused for at least a month, but we decided to try it anyway.

So next time we went off to "operetta practice," we let our dates bring us home by eleven, and we went up to our room and went to bed—clothes and all. Then, as soon as the housemother had made her bed check and was back in her room, we jumped up and stuffed our beds with pillows and wigs we had sneaked out of the cosmetology department—a light wig for Patty and dark for me. We put a chair outside the window and climbed out and ran across campus and out behind the hospital where our dates were waiting in the car. We ducked down, so we couldn't be spotted from any of the windows, and we were off!

We drove out around the lake, but we couldn't park out there because the cops came through every few minutes and flushed out the parked cars. So we drove around real slow a couple of times and headed back for the Pig Sty. That was the drive-in hamburger stand where all the kids hung out. We'd already been there once that evening, but back we went again. We got some more hamburgers and some more Cokes and turned the car radio up real loud and just hung around there. We lounged back in the seats and stuck our feet out over the doors and "lit up" which, for Patty and me, consisted of taking big, loud drags on a cigarette and exhaling through our mouths in big puffs, pretending we were smoking.

About two o'clock in the morning one of the boys fell asleep and the other one was nearly asleep, so they took us back behind our building and let us out. That's when the fun really began! Getting out had been easy, but now the gates were locked and there was no way in except up and over a five-foot chain-link fence. Patty stood on my knee, and she got over all right, but there was nothing for me to stand on. So I took hold of the fence post, pulled myself up as far as I could and did a forward somersault over the top.

That's how I tore my operetta costume! And wrecked the fence. And put a gash in my arm.

We sneaked across the campus all right, but just as we got up to the corner of our dorm, along came the night watchman. We dove into the bushes and laid low until his car had gone around to the other side of the square, then we climbed up on the chair and pulled it in after us. When we got into our room, we saw that Elvira was sound asleep, but Cory was gone. So we put the chair back outside the window and went to bed.

Ever since we had lived in the older dorms, we didn't have to line up for Manna Hall anymore, so while Patty and I were walking across campus on our way to breakfast next morning along came the night watchman.

"Good morning, Mr. Coleman," we said.

"Good morning," he said. "Well, I see you girls made it all right." He had been watching us from the minute we got out of that car and had come around to make sure we got inside safely.

One morning our school-bus driver was late, so we had to go over on the boys' side and board our bus next to the garage where it was parked. As we were backing out, I noticed a little gate next to the garage with one of those pull latches but no lock. Next time we sneaked off and stayed out late, we came around that way and tried the gate. Sure enough! There was no lock on it. We got in easily but it seemed like we crawled ten miles across campus, sneaking all the way over from the boys' side. And every time we did it, we felt sure Mr. Coleman was standing around somewhere, out of sight, watching us.

We didn't go out very often because of early-morning duties, but when we did, we stayed as late as we wanted. By that time, Patty and I had become very good at stuffing our beds. We'd bring colored wigs from the cosmetology department to match the current color of our hair, and we molded blankets and towels to look just like a person sleeping in that bed. Then off we'd go.

There were lots of kids who tried to run away from the Home, and it seemed that every morning the police were there with two or three kids they'd picked up and brought back. They never did seem to put two and two together, but the only girls who escaped were all in our dorm. Patty and I showed them how to do it. The ones who got caught and brought back were the ones that didn't have any place to go and no money to get there if they did. Once they got outside, they'd wander around looking lost and scared until somebody turned them in.

I guess that's why I never tried to run away, as badly as I wanted to get out of there. I had no place to go except to my Granny's and she'd only bring me back anyway. And by the time I was old enough to really plan something, I was getting out and doing all the things I wanted to do anyway, so there was no point in leaving.

One night we had gone to a late show at a drive-in and to an all-night drive-in restaurant after that. It was five in the morning and getting light when we came through the gate, and we barely had time to take a shower and get dressed before the first whistles would blow.

Patty and Cory were working in the kitchen that week so the housemother expected to hear water running at early-morning hours. But I was working in the hospital, and I had to help set up the breakfast trays. "Golly," I said to Velma, a girl who was working with me, "I'm so sleepy I don't know how I'll ever make it through school today."

"Here," she said, "take one of these. It's a diet pill. It gives you lots of pep and helps you stay awake." Well, one of the fellows had given me a NoDoz a couple of times, so I tried the diet pill. In about half an hour, I felt like I could run all the way to school.

"Wow!" I said to Velma. "That stuff really works! How do I get hold of some of those?"

"Go on a diet," she answered. "They let you eat all your meals over here when you're on a diet, and they give you these pills to help curb your appetite."

Well, that did it! Ever since I had gone over there to visit Patty while she was in the hospital, I'd been wishing I could eat over there. They had steaks and chops and all kinds of vegetables and sometimes they even had spaghetti which was my idea of ambrosia.

So I went on a diet and stayed on one from then until I left the Home, but I never did lose any weight. I ate the diet meals, but when I went to the kitchen to get something or to help clean up after a meal, I'd clean out all the spaghetti, mashed potatoes and gravy, apple cobbler, or practically anything that was left in a pan. But I got the diet pills. My first acquaintance with "uppers."

8

We're Free!

There were more than six hundred students in our high-school graduating class, and in spite of the way I felt about the Home, I felt a tingle of pride when the kids who had come from there were voted most friendly, most courteous, neatest dressed, and so on.

There was a graduation ceremony for us at the Home too, and once again my feelings were mixed. I felt hardened and rebellious, but I almost cried at the thought of leaving.

Each of us had a church or someone who sponsored us, and they gave us each fifty dollars, a whole new outfit of clothing, and a set of luggage. Some of our housemothers gave us little presents too; mostly things that they had made by hand.

And they didn't just turn us out to fend for ourselves. In addition to all those vocations we had learned by firsthand experience, they also took us on job interviews and got each one of us settled in something before they finally let go.

Some of the girls in our class passed their state-board exams and went into beauty shops. A few took up nursing, and Elvira went on to college. Some got jobs as secretaries and some of us wound up at the telephone company.

They dressed us up in our below-the-knee dresses and our matching hats, shoes, and purses. And they gave us each a pair of brand-new white gloves. We were taken to the phone company and sat down inside the office, all in a row, right where people were coming in to pay their bills. Well, those people walked in, glanced in our direction, then did a double take and stared. There we all sat in those wide-brimmed hats and white gloves, looking just like an Easter parade. We were so embarrassed. And we had to sit there so properly, not crossing our legs.

Mildred Hampton was fat, but she was about twenty-five pounds thinner than I was. When they turned her down, I thought, "Well, so much for the telephone company. Whadda we try next?"

But when it came my turn, they took me. I didn't know then that it was voice projection and enunciation that counted, not size. Score one for the Thespians and the school operettas!

They took Patty, too, so we got us a ninety-dollar-a-month efficiency apartment about two blocks from the phone company so we could walk to work. Two of Patty's aunts who had come for the graduation helped us move in. They said, "It looks like you girls need quite a few things," and they went out and bought us some pots and pans, a set of plastic dishes, and some stainless-steel knives, forks, and spoons.

The apartment was furnished, but not too well. It had a tiny kitchenette with a counter and stools, a pull-down bed, three chairs, two lamps, and a coffee table. In the cupboard, we found a cast-iron frying pan, a coffee pot, two paring knives, and a beer-can opener.

We unpacked our clothes out of our brand-new sets of luggage, put our big-brimmed hats, purses, and shoes on the closet shelf, and stowed all our personal things away in the drawers. We hung up our dresses, and then we took our brand-new white gloves and threw them in the garbage can.

On our very first payday, we went out and bought white jeans, white cashmere sweaters, and shiny white boots.

They had given us driver's education during our senior year at school, and Claudine had let me drive her car around until I could pass the test and get my driver's license. For graduation, she made the down payment on a new blue Barracuda with blue upholstery and turned it over to me.

After everyone had gone, we drove my new car to the nearest supermarket and loaded it up with groceries. We bought TV dinners, meat pies, spaghetti, a big sack of frozen french fries, cottage cheese, and steaks—all the things we didn't get at the Home—and then we stopped at a hot-dog stand on the way back and bought ourselves a couple of corn dogs, because I could never seem to get my fill of them.

We crammed the refrigerator with it all, opened a couple of Cokes, and started to cook our first meal. We were going to have corn dogs and spaghetti and french fries and ice cream! Well a big yellow moon started coming up over the horizon, so we took some more Cokes and went out on the balcony and started jumping around out there yelling, "We're free! We're free!" We ate the corn dogs, but the rest of our supper got cold, so our first meal in our new apartment consisted of corn dogs, Cokes, and ice cream.

Then we got in the car and started driving around, getting acquainted with our new neighborhood. When we came back, my watch and ring had been stolen.

My Granny had these two beautiful diamonds she had saved for a long time, and she had them set in a ring for me for graduation. I had laid the ring and my watch on the sink while I washed up the dishes, and when we came back, they were gone. After that, we were a little bit afraid about staying there at night, but we didn't get much sleep anyway, so it didn't matter after a while.

The phone company started us out on four-hour shifts. Four hours on and four hours off all around the clock. There wasn't much we could do in our four hours off except go to a movie or drive around, so that's what we did.

At first we'd spend most of the time hanging around the drive-in places trying to get some of the "cowboys" to notice us, then if a couple did come over to the car, we'd take off and spend the rest of the time trying to shake them.

For months and months it seemed like neither one of us got any sleep. First I'd sleep on the counter and Patty would sleep in the bed, then we'd switch around. We found out at once that we couldn't sleep together because we kept waking each other up saying, "Operator! Operator!"

When one of the girls at the phone company had all her money stolen and couldn't pay her rent, we invited her to come and stay with us until she could get some money saved again. She took one look around that tiny apartment and said cautiously, "Just where do you girls sleep?"

"Anywhere we can," Patty answered, so for three weeks, Nina took a pillow and two blankets and slept in the bathtub.

The guys at the bakery used to work at night too, so we started getting acquainted with them as we went back and forth to work, and before long, they were coming up to the apartment with a six-pack of Dr. Pepper, and we'd sit on the floor and listen to rock music on the radio and drink Dr. Pepper.

After a while, our hours got better at the phone company, and we didn't have to run back and forth all the time. We had struck up an acquaintance with some of the fellows who hung out at the beer joints, so sometimes they'd come over and we'd sit around and drink beer or go to a drive-in movie with them.

Whenever I had been out all night and didn't have any sleep, I'd just take a couple of my diet pills, and they'd get me through my shift. Some of the other girls at the phone company had what they called "uppers," and I'd borrow one or two of them when I felt draggy and run down. One of the girls had a doctor friend who would get them for us when we ran out.

It just seemed so great to be out of the Home and free to do whatever we wanted that we were going out or having people in almost every night. One of the fellows made delicious spaghetti, so sometimes we'd fix a big pot of it and sit around on the floor, eating spaghetti and listening to rock. Patty had a record player and albums of all our favorite rock groups. We'd sit around listening to Elvis or the Beatles half the night.

We had kept in touch with quite a few of the kids we had been friendly with at the Home, and one of the girls lived just five minutes away from us. She was going with a fellow who had been out at the Home, so sometimes they'd come over or we'd go over there and reminisce about the crazy things that had happened at the Home.

Whenever we went over to her house, there was this strange

smell like burning leaves or grass, and I often wondered what it was. One night when Patty was working late, I drove on over there with a pizza and some beer, and when I walked in, they were both smoking something that didn't smell like any cigarette I had ever smelled before.

"Hey, man," I said, "what're you guys smoking?"

"Marijuana," they said. "Here, try a joint."

Well by that time everybody'd heard of marijuana. It was hush-hush, but we all knew it was around. Well, I let them talk me into it. I smoked one but I didn't like the taste of it so after a couple of puffs, I went to the bathroom and flushed it down the toilet.

They started bringing it over to our place and passing it around. I'd take a couple of puffs and pretend I was high, because that's what they were doing, but it didn't have any effect on me at all.

Through hanging around with the guys from the beer joints, I had developed a real foul mouth. I had been warned about it several times by my supervisor when I said cuss words or worse under my breath and customers who had heard reported me. I was working as a long-distance operator then. The late hours and partying often made me very irritable the next day, so I was beginning to be short and sarcastic with the customers. Quite often I swore at them. But I was a union steward, and although the chief operator caught me many times, it took more than a few reprimands to get me fired.

Then one day a man swore at me for taking too long to put his call through, and I told him what he could do with it. That did it! They called me into the office and told me I was through. After I got through telling them what they could do with their job, it was a pretty sure thing that I'd never be able to work for them again.

I was still snorting and cussing about it that night when the grass-smoking kids from the Home came over. "Here," said Frank, handing me a pill, "try one of these. It'll calm you down."

I had tried all kinds of uppers and downers, and I thought this was just another one, but pretty soon I felt this strange tingling feeling starting at the base of my spine. I knew these kids were into acid—LSD—because some of the people we were hanging around with were getting it from them and were freaking out on it. But I hadn't tried it before then. I knew I had to be to work at a certain hour every day, and from what I could see, the acid eaters didn't have that kind of control over how far or how long the stuff would carry them.

Well tomorrow there wasn't going to be any job to worry about, so there wasn't any reason to hold out any longer.

One couple who were friends of friends were dabbling in yoga, and they would sit cross-legged on our floor and show us some of their exercises. They told us how the yogis would sit for hours and concentrate on certain places along the spine in order to "open" them to be aware of all kinds of things which couldn't be experienced with the normal senses. They talked about lights and colors and other levels of vibration, and they said acid got you there a whole lot faster.

I guessed that must be what was happening to me as I felt this sensation like a warm electric snake starting to crawl up my spine. But it stopped just below my shoulder blades and the tingling faded away into a dreamy, floating, contented feeling as though everything was all right with the world and there was nothing to get shook up about. When I looked at the lamps, I could see big circles of light with brilliant spokes of all kinds of colors spreading from the center outward in a kind of shimmering glow. Sometimes they were soft and pastel, and other times they were screamingly fluorescent, shifting in and out like the color on an out-of-focus TV.

As I really got into acid, I must have taken thousands of pills, sometimes twenty or thirty or more at a time. I heard all about kids who had walked out of high windows or burned out their minds completely. I saw a few go into crying jags and screaming, writhing fits, but I never had a bad trip or backflash of any kind.

I sincerely believe, with all my heart, that even way back then, the Lord had His hand on me.

When I woke up the the next morning, I was all alone. Patty had gone to work and everyone else had left too. I hauled myself to my feet and looked around. The apartment was a mess as usual: littered ashtrays, paper plates with bits of potato chips, pickles, and beer beans, records and album covers on the floor and coffee table, Coke bottles lying around. Yuck!

I dragged myself to the refrigerator for a Coke, but it was empty. The bean-encrusted pot was still on the stove. The big spoon we'd scooped them up with was lying in a drying puddle of juice beside it. There were dribbles on the stove, floor, and counter. I made a cup of coffee and tried to pull myself together.

And then it hit me! I didn't have a job. I wasn't going to have that weekly paycheck anymore. And nobody was going to pay my rent and feed my fat body for me. So I cleaned up the apartment and got dressed and went down to the unemployment office. I found out that what I could get out of them wasn't going to be very much, and even then, I'd have to wait two weeks before I could get my first check.

Patty was there when I got back to the apartment, and I told her what I had found out. "Golly!" she said, "How are we going to keep up the rent?"

"Yeah," I said. "And what about those monthly payments on my car?"

One of the fellows suggested I try to get a job as barmaid or cocktail waitress at one of the nearby joints. "You're real funny, Lu," he said. "And you're quick with the answers. You'd go over big in one of those places."

Yeah! Well, the first thing I found out was that you had to be twenty-one to work there, and I still had a while to go.

I tried to get a job as a regular waitress in some of the restaurants and hash houses. I even went out to one of the hospitals and tried to get into kitchen or cleanup work out there, but everywhere I went, they asked if I'd had any experience. The only experience I'd had was in telephone work and that was out! I couldn't even apply for switchboard, because the telephone company had written on my employment record, "Not recommended for rehiring."

And every time I got turned down at one of those places, I'd get farther and farther down in the dumps, so I'd come home and drop a couple of uppers or swallow some acid to get myself high again.

Well we only had a week left before we'd have to pay our rent again when the decision about whether we'd stay there or not was taken out of our hands.

Patty's father called. He was in what is called "remission"—a holding pattern in the progress of his disease—and he had taken the younger kids out of the Home and put them back in public school. The VA had increased his pension a little, and he was able to get some help from the county for the kids. He was asking Patty if she'd come and help him make a home for them. The clincher came when he told her that her mother was being released, too, and could come home if she had a home to come to.

"You can come and live with us!" Patty said, but when we drove over to the little house her Dad had rented, I saw that it was already a tight enough squeeze for the six of them. That night, our friends from the Home invited me to move in with them "until things got better," so I accepted their offer instead.

That's me, age six. I don't remember a great deal about the preschool dorm at the Home (behind me), but it was the beginning of a life regulated by whistles and bells and spent learning to obey the rules.

Christmas was the very best time, both at the Home and spent with Granny (right), who was strict with me but did what she thought was best, and "My Claudine," the one person I could always count on no matter what happened in my life.

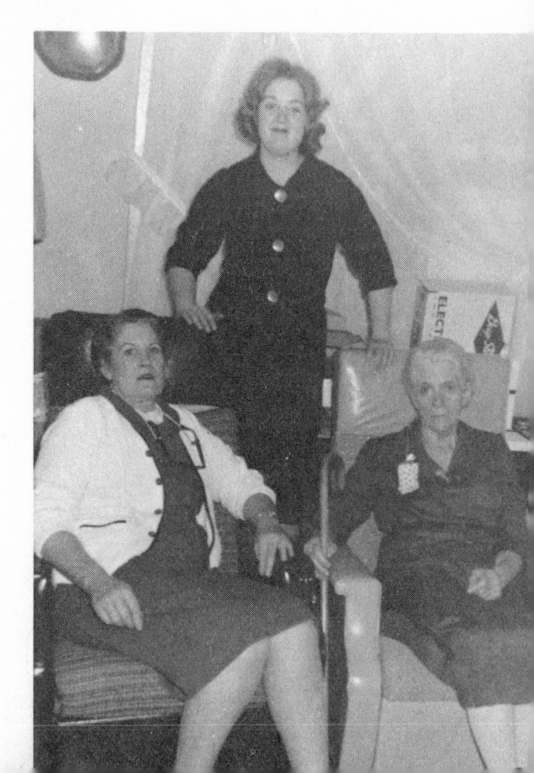

The greatest entertainer in the world—what more could I say about Roy Clark, "Hee Haw" host. *Left:* "LuLu has brought joy and happiness to so many people, and as someone who's proud to call her 'friend,' I'm glad she's found some of that joy for herself," said Buck Owens, "Hee Haw" co-star.

Grandpa Jones (left) and Orville find I always serve up a side order of laughs on "The Truck Stop" spot. (Photo by Sonny Brown) *Left:* Pat McCormick—Junior Samples—was part of one of the first sketches I ever did on "Hee Haw" and ever since we've been good friends.

What an honor to be on the same show with two of the sweetest people in show business—Roy Rogers and Dale Evans.

Jerry Reed got an armload when appearing as a guest star on ''Hee Haw.'' *Below:* Down home with ''The Culhanes'' (left to right), Gordie Tapp, Junior Samples, Grandpa Jones, me, and Kenny Price.

When I returned to the show after two years, the cast found this was definitely *not* the LuLu they had known! The coarse and cursing LuLu had completely disappeared. *Right:* "What happened? I met Jesus, and He's given me a new voice to tell His message and sing His praise," I told the "Hee Haw" cast as they couldn't believe I was going to sing—and a hymn no less.

I traveled with the Youth Crusade of America to Honolulu to join (left to right) Solomon Ono, Richard Shakarian, and Barry McGuire. I knew that out there in that sea of young faces were kids who needed to hear what I had to tell them about losing everything because of drugs. *Right:* "Boo" is what we call him, my son, Damon Erik, age five.

Since living at the Home, I have always cared about orphan children, and this concern was deepened when I traveled to Honduras with Frontline Ministries, a mission-assistance organization based in McAllen, Texas.

9

The Wrong Kind of People

Well things didn't get better. Instead they began to get infinitely worse. I had often thought it was odd that Frank and Barbara never said anything about where they were working, but it was a live-and-let-live relationship among the people we hung out with. Nobody asked personal questions of anybody else.

When I went to live with them, I found out why they never mentioned their jobs. They weren't working—not legitimately, at least. I discovered that instead of just smoking marijuana and popping acid pills, they were also handling the stuff. They'd get it in quantities, repackage it, and sell it for a profit. That's what they'd been doing in our apartment but even when I saw money change hands, I still hadn't realized what was going on.

But living right there with them, the way I was, I was soon weighing and measuring and counting right along with them. They let me go right on looking for a job once or twice a week, because that's what I had to do to keep drawing unemployment, but they wouldn't take any part of the little check I got to help with the living expenses. "That's all right," they'd say when I'd try to give them a few dollars now and then, "maybe someday we'll come and live with you."

Quite a few of the kids we'd known at the Home were hanging

around there, and one of them was Kenny, the kid I had dumped in the pool for smarting off at me about rescuing "Herman." Kenny was going with a girl from the Home who was a couple of years younger than we were. Her name was Sarah Jean, and she had been in the dorm with Patty's sister.

Kenny had always been a mean kid—sarcastic, tricky, and full of hurtful practical jokes. Instantly, upon leaving the Home, he got in with the wrong kind of people. He was in with a ring of people who were "hanging paper" as they called it—running credit cards and writing hot checks. They even had a money machine like one of those machines used to make money orders. They stole checks from some of the big factories and made them out to look like they were employee paychecks. They got thousands of dollars each payday by using several different names for each person and going to different supermarkets and stores to cash the checks.

I didn't get into that operation even though Barbara and Frank were a part of it, but I let Kenny talk me into buying things with a stolen credit card.

They stole people's mail and took their credit cards, and they had five of us girls who were running those stolen credit cards. We'd go into the stores several times a week and "buy" whatever we wanted by charging it on a credit card. Then we'd tear up the card before it was time for the person who owned it to get his bill.

There wasn't a limit on how much you could charge at that time, so we got everything. Televisions, radios, clocks, a washing machine, tires, shoes, clothing—everything!

Everything was going along fine until Kenny was in a big department store with me one day, and he decided he wanted a shotgun. I had the credit card, so I signed for the gun and while they were wrapping it up, I started walking around looking at the merchandise. Kenny saw the clerk take the card and go call on the phone, so he split. When I turned around and saw he was gone, I started to take off behind him, but the security guard had me before I got to the door.

"Whose credit card is this?" he asked.

"It's his, the man I was with."

"But you signed for it."

"Well, uh, he told me it belonged to his sister, and I could sign her name on it, because he didn't have his card with him."

"Where did he go?"

"I don't know. He must be here in the store somewhere. Maybe he went to the rest room." But, of course, he hadn't, and they couldn't find him. So they took me off to jail because I wouldn't change my story and wouldn't tell who it was that gave me the card.

It was my first offense, and I was still under twenty-one, so they let me off with two years' probation.

I was three months behind in my car payments and didn't know the finance company was looking for me, but they had spotters out trying to find my car. One night there came a rap on the door; they were there to repossess my car. Frank's car had a flat tire, and he had taken mine not ten minutes before and had gone off to meet his contact and pick up another delivery of the dope we were running. There was no way we could take a chance on having Frank drive up while those dudes were still there.

Kenny was in the next room, but he had gotten the picture real fast. His Porsche was parked out in front, so he went out the back door and around to the front to take off and ward off Frank, but one of the repossessors was out there, leaning against the car. Kenny went across the street to the beer joint, borrowed the keys to the bartender's car, went out the back door, and took off after Frank.

It was about three hours before they came walking across the street, where they had returned the bartender's car, and were carrying with them a whole load of stuff including the dope. Before they came back, they had taken my car way out in the country and had stripped everything off it that would come loose—tires, radio, headlights, hubcaps, antenna, sparkplugs, distributor—everything.

"You forgot the horn!" Sandy howled, when they dumped the stuff in the middle of the floor and told us what they had done.

Sandy and I were the only two girls in the crowd who didn't have any regular fellows, so we had started running around together. Sandy was tough. She was tall and thin with black hair and black eyes. She wore dark glasses and skin-tight black stretch pants that showed every pore in her skin, a tight black sweater, black boots, and black leather gloves. Sandy rode a motorcycle. Not one of those prissy little Hondas, but a great big Harley Davidson "hawg."

She would roar up to the house on that thing, park it out in back, and the two of us would make a round of the joints in my car. We had started to hang out at the bars, drinking beer, joshing with the fellows, and dating anybody who would take us out. But now we didn't have my car.

"Tell you what," Sandy said, "I've been telling you guys about Kelly. Why don't we all go down and catch her act?"

Kelly was the go-go dancer, "a real swell kid," who lived in the apartment next to Sandy.

Barbara and Frank said they couldn't go because they were expecting some folks in. That, in our parlance, meant they were going to make some sales, but Kenny said he'd take us down. Sarah Jean hadn't been around much lately. Kenny said she wasn't feeling well, but he had been hanging around more and more, making a strong play for me.

We got into his car and drove down to this place called the Icehouse. There were cars all over the parking lot, so we had to park about two blocks away.

I couldn't see a thing when we first went inside. There was a fellow up on a stage at one end, playing a guitar and singing an off-beat song. The whole place reeked of beer and cigarette smoke, but I was used to that. They led us to one little round table crowded between many others like it, and we ordered a round of beers. When my eyes got accustomed to the darkness, I saw that there were about a hundred of those tables each with candles in dark red shades. Every one of those tables was full, but besides Sandy and myself, I couldn't see more than three or four other women in the whole place.

The waiters were running around serving sandwiches and big glass mugs of beer when the three-piece combo started playing a hip-swinging tune. Immediately, the dudes went nearly crazy, stomping their feet, snapping their fingers, whistling and yelling, "Kelly! Kelly!" Then she came, a tiny Tinkerbell kind of a girl in sparkly high-heeled shoes, a sparkling band around her long golden ponytail and sparkling bikini. She had a beautiful face with big innocent-looking blue eyes, simply gorgeous legs, a soft, round, pattable bottom and the flattest chest I had ever seen. Just nothing. I wondered why she wore the top to that bikini when a couple of postage stamps would have done just as well.

But the dudes surely didn't seem to mind. She went into a slow, sensuous routine, with that ponytail swinging back and forth, and after the second or third verse, you could almost hear what she was singing. She did a real fast number after that, and I could see that she really did know how to dance.

Those guys wouldn't let her go. They whistled and stamped and yelled and brought her back for one encore after another. Finally the combo got up and left, and the lights were turned off on stage. After that the crowd quieted down. "C'mon back and meet her," Sandy said, so we inched our way through the tables and went backstage.

Kelly and I hit it off immediately. She was witty, sharp, and full of fun, and in five minutes or so we were throwing the jibes back and forth as if we'd known each other for ages. Kenny went completely ape over her, but she acted like she didn't even notice. We invited her to come back to the house with us after she was through, but she said she was busy so we went home.

As time went on, I saw that Kelly was busy most of the time, but Sandy and I started going over to her apartment in the late afternoons and hung around until it was time for her to leave for work. She had a gorgeous apartment: thick carpeting all over, a marble bathroom with huge plate-glass mirrors, an enormous bed with satin sheets and a beautiful cover with matching drapes at the windows. I had never seen anything so elegant in all my life. I thought that go-go dancing must really pay off, but when I said something like that to her, she just shrugged it off.

One afternoon while we were there, Kelly said she had to run down to the Icehouse to try out a new act and asked us to go along. That place sure looked different in the daytime—almost cruddy. I wouldn't have been surprised to see cockroaches crawling up the walls.

When we went in, the owner was sitting at one of those little tables, drinking beer with one of those Mafia types right out of the movies. Kelly told him why we were there, and he told her to go right ahead.

We went over by the stage, and she put on a record and started her new routine. Well it had some bumps and grinds, but the music was real catchy, and pretty soon I was on my feet imitating everything Kelly was doing. Sandy just started to howl. Then some guy who was mopping up came over and leaned on his mop to watch, and he began howling. Well, the owner and his Mafia-type friend turned around to watch, and pretty soon they were wiping their eyes and shaking their sides along with the others.

"Mutt and Jeff," somebody said, and we sure were. There was tiny little Kelly with no bosoms at all and here was big, fat me with a great deal more than plenty everywhere. While Kelly slithered and slid, I bounced, shook, made goo-goo eyes, and all kinds of facial distortions.

"You know somethin' girl?" the club owner said. "You're really funny. Tell you what I'm gonna do. You come down here and do that act with Kelly every night, and I'll give you a dollar a pound to be this town's biggest go-go dancer."

Well, now! That wasn't funny. At a dollar a pound, that figured out to about three hundred dollars a week, and I sure could use it. When I found out he was for real, I let out a wild "Yippee!" and treated everyone to a beer. Then I had to borrow money from Sandy to pay for it.

So that's what I did. I went down to the place five nights a week, and Kelly and I put on that crazy act. We did three shows a night, and we packed 'em in for every one of them.

When we started, I told Kelly that as soon as I got my first paycheck, I was going to look for an apartment of my own. Frank and Barbara had been awfully good to me, but I didn't want to impose on them any longer.

"Why don't you move in with me, Lu," Kelly said. "Please do. I get terribly lonesome, and we get along so well together. It wouldn't cost you anything for rent," she went on, "and you could get yourself another car."

Again I wondered about Kelly. The guys were crazy about her, but she never seemed to go out with anyone. Whenever Sandy and I went over to her place, she was always alone. She never talked about herself either, except in relation to her work at the club, but I just couldn't believe that was all the life she had.

The offer she had just made was too good to turn down, though. "Are you on the level?" I asked her.

"Really," she said. "I really am. I'd be very grateful if you'd move in with me. Most of the time I feel very scared, living there alone."

I decided to give it a try, so we went over in her Cadillac and picked up my things, and I moved into her apartment. "Well," I thought, looking around the big room she gave me, "you've finally made it, gal. This is really living!"

Four nights later, we were having a snack after coming home from the club about 3:00 A.M. when Kelly said, "Oh, I guess I better tell you. We're going to have company for a couple of days."

"Should I go over and stay with Frank and Barbara?" I asked.

"Oh, no," Kelly laughed. "There won't be anyone except Jim."

"Jim?" I said. "Who's Jim?"

"My special friend," she said. "This is his apartment. He lives in Chicago, but whenever he's down this way, he stays here."

So that was it! Suddenly all the pieces fell into place. Now I understood why Kelly was alone so much and why she didn't run around like the rest of us. She had a "sugar daddy!"

"Hey!" I said, "I'm getting out of here. Jim sure isn't going to like the idea of somebody else grazing on his spread!"

"Don't be silly," Kelly laughed. "Jim doesn't care what I do with the place or what I do, period, as long as I don't cheat on him and as long as I'm available when he's in town."

Well, she was right! He actually told me how glad he was that I had moved in with Kelly to keep her company when he was away! He took us to the club, picked us up when we were through, and even insisted that I go along to this fancy restaurant with them before we went to work one evening.

Jim was at least twenty years older than Kelly, and I guessed that he was married. He didn't seem to mind a bit that I was there, but even though I had my own room and bath I felt uncomfortable, so pretty soon, I got an apartment of my own nearby to get out from underfoot but still be near Kelly.

And pretty soon I was bored. So I called Sandy, and we went over to Frank and Barbara's, but this time we took Kelly along because Jim's "business trip" was over, and he had gone back to Chicago. She was bored, too. After that, whenever we went over there, or when we had parties in my apartment later, Kelly would drink beer or Cokes with us, but she never did smoke pot or drop acid with the rest of us. Later I found out why.

Kelly had been married to the son of a very socially prominent family, and she had two little children. One day she had come home unexpectedly and found her husband with another young man. She got a divorce and took her children to a small town in another state and gave them to her sister to raise. Kelly went to see them every few weeks, but she knew her life was nothing to get her kids involved in, so she was handling it this way. In spite of the club environment and the relationship with Jim, she never let herself get coarse in her language or her actions, and she never got into drugs. I admired her with all my heart.

We were doing pretty well for ourselves at the club, but the more things I had, the more I wanted, and I needed more money to buy them. So, before long, I was running dope again with Frank and Barbara. People started coming around to my place after we got off work, and they'd smoke pot or drop acid and freak out all over the place.

The joint Kelly and I were working in was pretty far down on the ladder, and Kelly wanted very much to get into the "big time," the night clubs and gambling places that were really high class and paid a lot more for entertainment. But with her little-boy front, she knew she'd never make it, so she was trying to save up enough for an operation that would build up her bust.

I had never been to any of the big-time clubs, so one night we decided to go. They had amateur night on Mondays at the club that was run by Ziggie, our boss's Mafia-type friend, and we didn't work on Mondays, so we went over. The place was packed, but Ziggie found a table for us and joined us when he wasn't busy.

That place was really something! Red velvet drapes on the stage, thick red carpeting on the floor, big paintings on the walls and a huge crystal chandelier. They had two or three regular acts and then they had an amateur-night contest. They picked girls out of the audience who wanted to be in it, and they gave the winner a seventy-five-dollar prize.

There were a couple hundred screaming females all waving their hands and yelling to be in the contest, but they only picked out ten. Then they took the contestants backstage, put some pasties on 'em, and had them come out and do their act. "My gawd!" I said to Ziggie, after the first six. "Those chicks are awful!" They had come out and wiggled around a little or else they had sung in high, squeaky voices or low, nasal voices, and you couldn't understand a word.

"Cheez," I went on, "as big as I am, I'll bet I could go up there and win that thing hands down!"

"I'll bet you can't," Ziggie said, pointing his faceful of big black cigar in my direction.

"How much?" I asked.

"Twenty-five bucks," he said, "in addition to the prize."

"You're on," I said. "I'll be back next Monday night. Better get yourself a coupla hubcaps, 'cause I'm gonna win that son of a gun."

I went to a costume-rental place and got myself a big pair of black and white polka-dot bloomers like the ones clowns wear in parades. I put a big red bow in my hair and another one on the back of the bloomers. I put a bicycle lock on the front and got a pair of big lace paper doilies and one of those great big all-day suckers, and I went on stage.

And for the first time in my life I was petrified!

I looked down at that sea of unsmiling faces, and I didn't know what to say or do. So I just stood there licking that big sucker and rolling my eyes. Then somebody snickered. And somebody else guffawed. It started at the front and went toward the back, like a slow-burning fuse, but in a couple of minutes the whole place was laughing.

On purpose, I dropped my sucker on the floor. Then I turned my back to the audience and bent over to pick it up with my feet spread wide apart like I had seen the clowns do in the circus. When the crowd saw the big red bow on my fanny, they jeered and guffawed and howled. I peeked out at them from between my legs, straightened up, turned around, wiped the sucker off on the seat of my pants, and went back to licking it again.

Then I pretended I was trying to find a place to put the sucker while I went into my dance. I showed the crowd there were no pockets in the bloomers and then I went through the motions of starting to pull off one of the doilies to park the sucker on it. "G'wan! Pull it off!" the dudes hollered, but I walked to the front of the stage instead and borrowed a sheet of music from one of the orchestra fellows. As I laid the sucker down on that and straightened up again, some guy down in front yelled, "Hey, LuLu, where'd you get the bicycle lock?"

"My mama gave it to me," I answered in a little-girl voice, "so's I wouldn't peddle." After about five minutes or so of that kind of exchange, I finally went into my dance.

The crowd loved it. They went wild. They stamped and whistled and yelled and, like I had told Ziggie, I won the son of a gun hands down. "You wanna come back," Ziggie said as he gave me the prize money and paid off his bet. "I'll make it worth your while." So every Monday night for a while, I went down there and "won" that amateur contest.

Pretty soon the word got around and before long some of the other club owners were making it worth my while to do my act in their clubs too. Kelly and I weren't working together right then, so I accepted their offers. Jim had come into town again, and I had let the word drop that Kelly wanted to buy some bosoms. "Golly, honey," Jim told her, "if you're sure that's what you want, I'll pay for the operation."

Well Kelly went through hell! None of the ads she had read said anything about the physical torture connected with that kind of surgery, but she suffered something awful. Months and months later, I asked her one day if she thought it was worth it. "I guess so," she said somewhat doubtfully, "but I never in all this world would go through a thing like that again."

In the meantime, I was doing the rounds of the clubs. I had it fixed so I'd go do my act in one of them, then get out and go do it at the next instead of doing two or three shows a night in one club. I could make more money in one night that way, than the other girls were making in a week, by just doing those spot shows.

At first it was fun, but after a while it got to be a big bore. I'd go and do what I had to do and get out. I wouldn't talk to anyone or hang around a minute longer than I had to. When I was through, I'd go home and get high with my friends.

Most of the people where Kelly and I lived were partying people, folks who worked at night in the clubs or did something like we did. Sometimes we'd get together around the pool and cook beer beans or have a barbecue and sing and dance and carry on, but most of the time we'd just get high on dope and see who would crash out first on the floor. I can remember waking up and finding two or three people freaked out on my floor, and I didn't even know who they were.

We'd have these late, late parties two or three nights a week. The club owners and everybody would come over, sit around and listen to heavy music on the stereo, and get stoned. And it got to the point where the narcotics officers were following me home. They were wise to any girl who was working in the clubs, because they knew that they had to be involved with dope or something illegal.

They'd follow me home and pull their car up next to mine and yell, "Hi, Lu! You holding tonight?" And I'd yell back, "Git away from me, man. I haven't got any dope on me!" Sometimes I wouldn't even be out of my car, before they'd be out of theirs and starting to search my car. But I was so sharp and so slick by then that they even raided my apartment two or three times, but they never found a thing.

One night they came in and tried to bust the party. They didn't get me for anything because they didn't find any dope in my house, but they found a gun on one of the fellows, and they took him away for that. I remember one of the officers had gone into the bathroom, and he found some sleeping pills that didn't have any label on them. He was going to take me down to jail for that, but the other officer talked him out of it. He took me into the bathroom, and he said, "All right. I'm going to give you a chance, Lu. You know I could bust you for this." So he took the pills and flushed them down the toilet. Then he said, "All right, girl, straighten up." And they left.

I had never expected to get any kind of a break from the "fuzz" that was following me around night after night, and I thought about that for a while, but not long enough or deep enough. Pretty soon I was right out there getting high with everybody else again.

Sandy and some of her friends were among the regulars who kept on dropping in at my place, so one night they came over and along with them came this stranger. He was tall, dark, handsome, with warm brown eyes and flashing white teeth—the handsomest guy I had ever seen off the screen, and he took me in completely. No matter how many dudes hung around my place or anywhere else that I went, I never lost my cool over any of them, but I fell for Harry—hard—the moment I saw him. And I made up my mind I was going to have him, even before he was all the way into the room.

When he stood near me, I felt a warm glow all over. When he touched my hand, I felt a thrill I had never gotten from dope, no matter how much of it I took.

Before long, Harry moved in, and I was happier than I had ever been in my life. He ran my errands, waited on me hand and foot, took me to work and picked me up when I was through, and I never even noticed that I was supporting him.

Then one night there was a fire at the last club on my circuit, and they phoned where I was to let me know the show wouldn't go on. I thought I'd surprise Harry, so I rode home with a couple of guitar players who lived in our building. My big black Continental was parked outside waiting for Harry to come to work and get me, so I knew he was home.

Very quietly, I let myself in with my key, and there was Harry, in my bed with another girl.

I went right out of my gourd! Shrieking the foulest words I could think of, I picked up a heavy brass candlestick and charged them both. The girl streaked across the apartment, out the front door and along the balcony, completely naked. I chased her all the way to the stairs, hurling every cussword in my book. I never did know what happened to her. I never asked.

When I got back to the apartment, Harry had pulled on his pants and was reaching for his shoes. I went after him with the candlestick, and he picked up his shoes and ran. "Don't you ever come near me again, you double-dealing, low-down so-and-so,'' I screamed after him. When I went downstairs much later, I discovered he had taken my Continental and left.

I went into the bathroom and downed fifteen acid pills, three and four at a time. When they started to hit me, I laid down spread eagle on the floor and drifted away, hoping I'd never wake up, but when I did, Sandy was sitting on the couch staring at me.

I lay there, letting it all fall down around me bit by bit, and when I could piece it all together again, I sat up and dumped the whole mess in Sandy's lap.

''I guess I should have warned you,'' she said, ''but I thought you were big enough to take care of yourself. Harry's like that. He's a tremendously talented guy. He can do just about everything, but he lives off women. They just fall apart at the seams over him, and, well, I guess he doesn't put up any resistance.''

Okay! So I had learned that lesson. I called the Salvation Army and gave them my bed. I certainly wasn't going to sleep in it again! Then I went out and bought myself a new one.

I went back to work the next night, but I hated it. I hated everything I was doing, and I hated everything I was. I was sick of the whole messy business, so I went to work and came home and hit the dope harder than ever.

By that time they were billing me as *LuLu Roman* all over town. Whenever I had gone on stage with Kelly at that first place where we worked, some dude was sure to holler out, ''She's a lulu, all right,'' and pretty soon it stuck. I added *Roman* because it was Latin sounding and seemed to go with my black hair.

One day I was sitting in front of my dressing table staring at the bulbous pulpy mass that stared back at me. Disgusted, heartsick, as low down as I'd ever been—''Dear God,'' I said, ''please get me out of this mess.''

If that was a prayer, it was the first one I'd uttered since I was in sixth grade, but I believe, like the song says, that ''Someone up there hears every word,'' and I know He must have heard that one too.

10

They're Going to Call It "Hee Haw"

One afternoon a couple of days later, I was in the bathtub when the phone rang, and it was Buck Owen's manager.

"Hi, Lu," he said, "What're you doing?"

"What'm I doing?" I said. "Man, I'm in the bathtub. When're you coming to town?"

"I'm not coming to town," he said. "I'm in Canada."

"Let me figure this out," I said. "You're in Canada, and you're calling me, and you're not coming to town. Is something wrong up there?"

"No. Nothing's wrong," he said. "Listen. You remember how I've always been telling you how funny you are, and that you'll be in a show one day, and I'll have something to do with it?"

Yeah. I remembered. He'd been telling me that for a couple of years. One night while Kelly and I were still doing our act, Kenny had come around and had asked Kelly and Sandy and me to a party. "Buck Owen and some of his gang are going to be there," he said, "and a lotta other folks, and you're invited if you want to go."

Well we got all dressed up, went over to this place, and there wasn't anybody there but Buck Owen and his boys. Kenny had known they were going to be there and this was his idea of a joke.

Or maybe his idea of getting even with me for not cozying up to him like he wanted.

Anyway we were about to go back home, but they invited us in. So we sat and talked, had a few beers, and got to be real good friends. After that, whenever they were in town, they'd call up and say, "C'mon over and see the show, and we'll have supper." That had gone on for quite a while.

Only this time they weren't in town, and I still didn't know why he was calling from Canada.

"Hey, gal," he was saying, "I've got some good news! Some people I know are putting together a country-western comedy show. It's kind of a cornball answer to 'Laugh In,' and they want you to be the Goldie Hawn."

"Goldie Hawn!" I shrieked. "Isn't she that little bitty skinny blond?"

"That's right," he said. "They're looking for somebody to be her opposite." I found out later that they had asked him if he knew a big dumb broad with black hair.

"Well," I said, "I guess they just found her. Where are they going to put on this show?"

"On television," he said. "They're going to call it 'Hee Haw.' It's going to be a series on nationwide television like 'Laugh In' used to be."

Right away, all I could see was dollar signs, bing, bing, bing, so I said, "All right. What do I have to do?"

They sent me tickets, and I flew to Hollywood. Buck and his manager met me at the airport and took me to CBS Studios. To me, it looked like a great big barn with lights and wires and scaffolding all over. Well they showed me around there, and I met some of the stars I'd seen on television. I thought, *Wow! Little orphan girl really makes good. I wonder what the kids at the Home would say if they could see me now!*

We went into the wardrobe department, and they put me in a pink dress with ruffles and big buttons, the one Jonathan Winters used to wear. Then they stood me in front of a camera and handed me a script and said, "Here, little girl, read this." So I read it, and they said, "Hey! You're really good!"

I said, "Gimme your money, and I'll be better." That's all I could think about at the time. Money was my god. Money bought the things I wanted. Money got me friends.

The next day they took Pat McCormick and me over to Griffith Park, and we did a takeoff on the Clairol commercial where a girl and a fellow run toward each other in slow motion. Her hair is flying in the breeze, and it's all diffused and very romantic. Well, I was barefoot and making funny faces, and Pat was in bib overalls and panting with his tongue lolling out. We came galloping toward each other like two overeager hounds, and when we came together, we bumped stomachs and fell down.

When we got up to the studio in Nashville, I was thinking about all this goofy cornball stuff we had done, and I thought, *I know Buck Owen is real popular, and I know Roy Clark is very well known, too, but I can't believe anybody's going to watch this garbage.*

But they did! "Hee Haw" hit the number-one spot almost overnight and just stayed right there on the TV ratings.

I went up to Nashville and filmed the shows with them. They gave me my money, and I bought everything I'd always wanted. I bought another Continental and a very nice three-bedroom house. I furnished it with all the stuff I could find that I thought was really "cool": big psychedelic posters and those crazy flashing lamps, a stereo, astrological charts and emblems, big soft rugs, huge pillows, low tables, and a water bed.

I bought my friends. I bought their time, their food, and their dope, and one day I got to thinking that with all this money, I could get it wholesale and cut it and sell it the way Frank and Barbara were doing. So I went over and talked to them about it, and I started buying large amounts of it through them.

We'd get a delivery of marijuana like a big bunch of dried green leaves, and we'd bag up "lids" of marijuana in little baggies and sell it. A "lid" is about four fingers wide, and we'd sell it for fifteen dollars. The marijuana wasn't always green. Sometimes we'd get Acapulco Gold which was gold colored and sometimes we'd get Panama Red which was red colored. It all depended on what part of the country the dope was grown in. And the potency was just unbelievable. I'd smoke this stuff, and become very, very stoned. It made me feel light headed and very happy, like I didn't have a care in the world. It dulled my senses, so my nerves weren't on edge. I moved around in a sort of slow-motion world. My reactions were slowed down and certainly not as sharp as they should have been especially when I was driving, but I felt relaxed, pleasantly hazy, slowed down, and mellow.

I had started out on marijuana, as a weekend tripper, when I was working for the telephone company, and I never had any sign of a reaction. That made it easier to get into it more and more and to try other things like acid later on. If I'd ever had any side effects or aftereffect, if I had ever had a bad trip or had come out of it all shaken and jangling, I might have stopped, but it was never like that for me—just a warm, soft, fuzzy, hazy kind of feeling.

One day I had just slipped back into that world when the doorbell rang. The lights were turned down, the stereo was turned up, the air was filled with blue smoke, and I was lying on the floor in the middle of this big, soft, white, shaggy rug, just floating and listening to the music. Somehow I managed to pull myself together and get to my feet. I struggled into a robe and went to the door. There stood Harry.

"Oh, baby," he said, in that deep, rich voice of his. "Oh, honey, I've missed you something awful!"

I should have slammed the door in his face, but I was too misty, too far out of it to think. I had missed him something awful, too, and while I stood there befuddled and not saying anything, he came inside and put his arms around me. Even through the haze of all the dope, I knew that was what I wanted more than anything in the world.

After a while, we were both lying there on the rug. Contented, drifting, floating away on a big white cloud. I couldn't analyze it or think it through. I couldn't even follow one simple thought all the way through to a period. All I could do was feel, and right then I felt all the things I had ever imagined heaven to be.

Well, Harry moved in again, and I let it happen. In my more rational moments, I knew he had running blood. I knew he had probably come back because he'd heard about "Hee Haw" and he knew I was making it big. I knew he'd never be true to any woman, and he'd probably stick around only as long as the money held out. But I didn't think there would ever be an end to the money—not as long as I kept running up to Nashville every few months and doing those "Hee Haw" shows and not as long as I kept buying those quantities of dope and selling it for about four times as much as I paid for it.

There had been other men in my life after Harry left. I had three or four of them crashing my pad all the time, but I had less feeling for them than I would have had for a pack of dogs. I kept them around for companionship, because I couldn't stand to be alone. Now that Harry was back, I ran them all off and let them go find someone else to pay their rent and buy their dope. But the partying went on as before. Ten, fifteen, twenty people or more hanging around night after night. Dropping acid, smoking pot, lying around listening to heavy music, and seeing who would crash first.

I thought this was it, man! I had this beautiful home, my big Continental, all these friends, and all this fun, and I was getting a little fame as a television star also. This was what it was all about. This was really the big time.

It went along that way for about three years. The "Hee Haw" people knew I had problems. They could hardly get away from the trashy mouth. They knew about the drugs, too, but they didn't know how to handle it. So they just let it go along until I played the wrong card and I watched my whole life come tumbling down around me.

One afternoon Sandy and some of her friends dropped in with a new rock album, and we were sitting around there popping pills and listening to that album. There was a bathroom right off the kitchen, and I was in there when Sandy came into the kitchen for a Coke. "Hey, Lu," she called out, "Kelly's opening at the Club Continental tonight. Wanna go along with us and watch her show off her new boobs? She's been working on this new act for a coupla months, y'know."

"Oh, darn," I yelled back, "I'd sure like to, but Harry's taking a pound over to Blue Ridge, and we've got this shipment coming around eight-thirty. Maybe I can drive over after that if there aren't too many people hangin' around here by then."

"Okay," she said. As I opened the door and walked into the

kitchen, I saw this dude going through the door into the living room with two Cokes and two glasses, but I didn't think anything of it at the time—not until later that evening. He was comparatively new around my place. Some junkie Sandy had met in a bar somewhere, I thought.

Well when the delivery was made that evening, the narcotics officers came right behind it. That dirty squealer had left my place that afternoon and had tipped them off. Actually, he had hung around there for weeks, finding out who came in and out regularly, following them home and then working out this "chance" meeting with Sandy and growing on her until she finally brought him along a few times.

So I was standing there with five and one-half pounds of marijuana when they walked in. I didn't even have time to put it up in the cupboards. They tore the place to shreds, and they found acid, speed, needles, just name it. While the cops were there, Barbara and Frank walked in, and the officers tried to get them in on the bust too. But we all played it very cool, and I was able to convince them that Barbara and Frank had nothing to do with it.

Through all of my problems, Sharon—along with Claudine—had been one of the most loyal and true friends I've ever had. Sharon had gone to school to learn bartending, and she could run a whole joint by herself, but she stuck with bartending and being a cocktail waitress.

When they took me to jail, the one call I was allowed to make, I made to Sharon. We had keys to each other's houses, so I told her they had missed some stuff in my cupboards, and I told her to go home and clean it out and to be sure and clean her house too. I knew if they got on one of those raiding streaks, they might get her on Valiums or anything they found. I had four bottles of liquid speed they had gone right over—didn't even see—and I didn't want them to go back and find them.

My lawyer came down and got me out on a writ of habeas corpus, and I thought, *Hmph! I'm LuLu Roman! I've got money; I can buy my way out of this.* I had no idea how long and how torturously they could drag it out. I went to court eleven times during the next two years. The first time, I came away with a mistrial. I'd already had one probated sentence on the stolen-credit-card rap, so I couldn't get probation again, but it didn't seem to bother me any. All the time I kept on being very smug about it and thinking I could buy my way out of it.

We hired one of the best lawyers in the state. He won nine out of ten cases, but he lost mine. I thought we could buy anything. I thought I could buy judges and juries, but I couldn't. The second time in court, I came away with a verdict of guilty, and I was sentenced to four years in the penitentiary. I appealed the case and sent it to the state capital, so I could buy some time. I still thought I'd get out of it.

When I came home that first day, after they had raided my house and found me with all the marijuana, there was nobody around. I went into the bedroom and all Harry's things were gone. He had just disappeared. Apparently the low-down stool pigeon that turned me in had told the undercover men everything, because all through the trial, they kept referring to a man named Harry, but I acted like I'd never heard of him. They weren't able to find him. I was so miserable that I couldn't help myself, so I just went right on doing what I'd been doing, getting high and staying high, so I didn't have to think about anything.

Then the time came and went by for the "Hee Haw" people to do their next taping, and I didn't hear a word. Finally, one day I got a call. It was the producer, and he was so kind and so sorry, but there wasn't a thing they could do. The publicity had grown to such proportions as my case was dragged in and out of court that they just had to go on without me. That kind of publicity could lose them their show.

I was so depressed that I just kept on taking more and more dope to pull myself out of it. I didn't want to do anything but get high so I could forget about my troubles. I thought this was the worst thing that could possibly happen, but I was so wrong. This was low blow number two, but number three was already standing in my door.

11

My Baby! He Must Be Dead!

I had been feeling something different and peculiar inside of me for a couple of weeks, and there were other indications that something was wrong, so I finally went to the doctor. When the examination was over, he told me I was about two months pregnant.

Ever since I'd been at the Home, I had this thing against marriage. My feelings about it were all mixed up with the *thou shalt nots* they had thundered at us for so many years. I suppose that being against marriage was one of my ways of expressing defiance toward it all. But I still believed that I had a "God-given right" to have children if I wanted to.

"No slip of paper can give me the right to have babies," I used to say. "That right isn't granted by the establishment. It comes straight from God, and I was born with it. Nobody can tell me whether I can or can't be a mother!"

Well, now I was going to be, and I was scared!

The first thing I did when I got home from the doctor's was to go to Sharon's. She knew what this business was all about! Sharon had two little girls but, like Kelly, she didn't want them mixed up in the kind of life she was leading. In addition to being a bartender and cocktail waitress, Sharon also had a couple of wealthy men who supported her, so her girls were being raised by their grandmother.

In a situation like mine, she didn't know whether to be glad or sorry, so she just said, "Hmmm. That's interesting," when I told her the news. "Are you going to tell Harry?" she asked, pouring me a Coke.

"I will when he turns up again," I said. I knew he'd come back to me sooner or later, and I felt sure he'd be glad to know we were going to have a child.

Sometime later, I was driving along the street one day when I saw him on the sidewalk. I pulled over, and he got in the car.

"Oh, Lu, baby," he said, "I've missed you something awful!"

"Yeah!" I said sarcastically. "I can tell."

"But, honey," he said, "you don't understand," and even though something inside me told me it was just another con game, I swallowed everything he had to say for one more time.

When he came back from Blue Ridge that night and saw the cops were there, he just made a U turn in the middle of the street and kept right on going.

"I couldn't come back," he said. "You know there's a warrant out for my arrest too. I couldn't even call you, because they might have your phone bugged. I've been watching the papers, and with your being dragged into court and all, I thought I'd just better stay away until this whole thing cools down. Besides," he went on, "somebody's got to stay loose on the outside to keep our contacts open."

He went home with me, anyway, and after a while, when we were sitting on the couch, I told him about the baby. "Oh, wow!" he said in a kind of awed and reverent tone of voice, and he seemed to be very happy about it. But he left soon after that, and it was three weeks before I heard from him again.

He called one afternoon and asked if he could come over and everything seemed to be all right while he was there, but as time went on, he just drifted away, and I didn't see or hear from him at all.

Then one night, when I was about seven months pregnant, I went with a friend to one of the clubs to see one of his friends who was performing there.

We went in and sat at one of the tables, and after a while, who should come in but Harry. After his eyes got accustomed to the darkness, he looked over and saw us sitting there, and without so much as a nod, he got up very quickly and left. I tried to tell myself that maybe he hadn't seen me or maybe he'd left on his car lights or all kinds of crazy things, but inwardly I was feeling pretty sick. Finally I told my friend Don, "Look, I gotta get out of here for a little while, okay?" so we got up and went next door and just stood there in the shadows.

Well, it worked. In a few minutes, Harry came in again. He thought we had left, and so he was going back into the club again. I'd heard from several of my friends, girls in particular, that he was telling everyone around town that LuLu needn't think she was going to hang this brat on him. Now that he was really avoiding me, my heart told me what they said was true.

Shaking with grief, anger, fear, and bitterness, all mixed up together, I confronted him in the doorway and said his name. Well, with big Don standing there beside me, he didn't have any choice except to stand there and talk. I told him what I'd heard, and he put his hands on my now very swollen stomach and said, "Lu, I really wish it was my baby, but you know darn well it ain't."

This was about the last rejection I could take. I stood there with tears streaming down my face and said, "Harry, God in heaven knows this seed was put here by you, but this baby is mine. Mine alone. Don't you ever try to lay claim to it, ever! Anyway, I wouldn't want my child to know what a worthless s.o.b. his father is!"

He looked shocked for a moment, then he turned and went on into the club. Hurt, angry, and humiliated, I stood there sobbing. Then Don led me to the car and took me home. It was years later before I saw Harry again.

When I was a little kid I used to long to have someone put their arms around me and say, "I love you," but no one ever did that for me at the Home. I'm sure many of the housemothers loved us, but there were far too many of us, and they were all too busy. Some of the housemothers had been very kind and understanding, but none of them had ever held me close and secure and said, "I love you." Right now, my whole being yearned for that kind of love. I had tried to find a substitute for it through sex and drugs, but there was no substitute. I had tried to buy it with money and gifts and favors, but it couldn't be bought.

It was the kind of love I used to think I would feel from my mother if we'd ever had a chance to have a warm and loving relationship. It was the kind of love I'd want to give my own baby, but now . . . oh, dear God, would he have to grow up in an orphanage, too? What would I do with him if I had to go to jail? I couldn't let him go to the Home. I wouldn't inflict that kind of life on any child if I could help it.

I got out of Don's car and crawled into the house, numb, desperate, not wanting to believe it had really happened. Over and over again, Harry had told me how much he loved me. Now he was disowning his own child. I kept trying to make believe that it was all a bad trip, that it hadn't really happened, and I'd come out of it after a while. But part of me really knew better. I had swallowed dozens of acid pills all at one time just to see how high I could get, and I'd never been on a bad trip in my life.

No, it was true all right and after a while I forced myself to face the horrible mess I had made of my life. Back at the Home, I used to say that if I ever got out of there I was going to do everything they'd told me not to do—at least once. Well, I'd done it, and now I was in deeper than I ever dreamed I could get. I felt desperate, trapped, achingly lonely, and scared.

Desperate and sick with a gnawing, burning fear like I'd never felt in my life, I went into the bathroom, looking for somthing to wipe out all the misery and pain. I always had a good supply of tranquilizers on hand. That way, if I got too wired up or too buzzy, I could take some tranquilizers and settle down and go to sleep.

Standing there, staring at the pills in their little glass bottles, I couldn't see any reason to go on living. There wasn't any future in it as far as I was concerned. Just the same old grind of swallowing pills to get high and swallowing more pills to get down and of wallowing around night after night with a bunch of bums who only wanted sex as a scratch for the place that itched.

And jail. Why should I hang around and let them throw me in jail? I'd have my face smeared all over the smutty newspaper pages. LULU ROMAN, STAR OF "HEE HAW," GOES TO JAIL. No thanks. Not while I could make my exit whenever I wanted to. The baby? What could I offer him if I wasn't even going to be around to take care of him? A foster home? Growing up in an orphanage the way I had? Uh uh! If he were never born, he'd never have to die.

I poured all sixteen "red birds"—Seconal—into my hand. Next I took the top off of a bottle of "blues"—ten milligram Valiums—and added about thirty of those to the fistful. Down they went, plop, plop, as many as I could swallow at a time. Then I went into the living room and turned on some heavy music on the stereo and laid down on the couch and waited for all those pills to take effect.

The next thing I knew, I was floating back up to consciousness, and I kept right on going, up and up and up. I came out of it feeling higher and more "all's right with the world" than I could ever remember feeling before. Wow! What had I gotten hold of anyway? I thought I'd overdosed with sleeping pills but some dude must have put something else in the bottles. No. They *were* reds and blues. I remembered emptying the bottles. But what happened? How come I felt so high?

I opened my eyes and there was Sharon bending over me with a needle in her hand. "You didn't . . ." I started to say.

"Yes, I did," she said. "I came in here, and you were out on the couch, and I couldn't rouse you. When I went into the bathroom I found those empty bottles. I was afraid you'd OD'd, so I shot you with a hit of speed to see if it would bring you out of it. Thank God it did."

That's what Sharon was into. She'd had a row with the man she was living with a while back, and he walked out on her. When she was despondent at the hotel where she was tending bar, one of the fellows who worked there persuaded her to let him give her a "hit" to see her through the night. But one hit was all it took, and now she was hooked on it. And now she had just pumped enough of it into my arm to counteract all those "downers" I had taken, so I must be hooked, too.

But I didn't care. I felt great! I was happy! I felt like everything was going to turn out just dandy, and I didn't have a care in the world. *Man!* I thought. *If this is what speed can do, just give me the needle and get out of my way!*

I'd never gotten involved with that stuff before. There were people all over my place, sticking needles into their arms, but needles just scared the fire out of me. Now I found out what I was missing, so I became a "speed freak" too. And that's what I did all the while I was pregnant. I shot myself so full of holes that the veins in my upper arm collapsed and I had to shoot it into my wrist and the back of my hand, but I didn't care just as long as I could stay high and happy and not have to face the ugly realities of the real world.

By this time Sharon was living with me. She couldn't make the payments on her place after her "sugar daddy" walked out, so she moved in with me. I collected unemployment insurance off of "Hee Haw," and we sold dope. That's how we made our living.

We had very good "connections" through a friend who had worked in a doctor's office, and we were getting 96 percent pure methedrine. It came in a white powder, and we mixed it about half and half with baking soda and packaged it in those little coin bags. A dime bag sold for ten dollars, a quarter bag sold for twenty-five dollars, and a half-dollar bag sold for fifty dollars. Out of the ten-dollar bag, you could get one good "hit," and out of the twenty-five-dollar bag, you could get, maybe, four "hits." So, if a person needed only one "hit" a day, it would still take him about seventy dollars a week to "live."

Sharon had not been involved in "trafficking" before, but now we were both involved in it right up to our eyeballs. I watched my money dwindle away, and the "friends" who had hung around because of it all slunk away too. Then, when I couldn't make the payments on the house, they came and repossessed that, and Sharon and I moved into an apartment.

The people who lived around us were all "hippies" and "freakies" like we were. So pretty soon they were coming in and bringing their friends, and we were selling dope to them and pumping it into ourselves. That's how I lived, right up to the day my baby was born.

Then, on the night I went to the hospital, someone stole my car right out of the parking lot and drove it clear across town. When the police found it a week or so later, everything that would come loose had been stripped off it.

Earlier that day I got up from the couch where I had been sitting, and I felt this very sharp pain in my side, just as though someone had stuck me with a knife. After a while, came another one and that kept on every half hour or so for a few hours. Then they started coming about every fifteen minutes.

Sharon had been off somewhere, so when she came home I told her about it. "I've been getting these sharp shooting pains in my side," I told her. "They started about two o'clock, and they've been getting worse. Do you think I could have appendicitis?"

"Where is the pain?" she asked.

"Here," I said, holding my hand just below my ribs on the left side.

"You're probably in labor," Sharon said, "because, unless you're different from everybody else, your appendix is on the other side. Just how often have you been getting these pains?"

"They seem to be coming more often now," I told her, "maybe fifteen minutes or so apart, but it isn't labor. You're supposed to have a backache with that, and it's my side that's killing me."

"Look, kiddo," she said, "you ask ten different women about labor, and you'll get fifteen different descriptions. Take it from me, you're in labor. Now go get your bag packed, so I can take you to the hospital before I have to go to work."

She took me to the hospital in my car. Then after work she came back to the hospital and walked the floor with me. And sometime before dawn my car was stolen. I realized that this latest blow meant I was going to have to rely completely upon somebody else for transportation, but I had far bigger worries to think about just then.

When I got to the hospital, they confirmed that I was in labor all right. They put me in a bed, but I couldn't stay in it. It seemed to help, when the contractions came, to be up on my feet, so I walked. Then the bleeding started, so they shoved me back in bed again and said, "Stay there!," but I couldn't stand it. When Sharon got there about 3:00 A.M., I was pacing up and down the room, moaning, screaming, wailing, and bleeding.

Sharon had been through this twice, and she also knew it wouldn't do any good to tell me to stay in bed if I didn't want to, so she got something to sop up the bleeding and then she grabbed my hand and just paced around the room with me. Finally, when I squeezed her hand so hard that I almost cracked her knuckles, she got a towel from the bathroom, tied a knot in it, and said, "Here! When the pains come, bite on this!"

Finally, about 8:30 in the morning, they said they were just going to have to take the baby, and I said okay. So they took me into the operating room, and instead of doing a cesarean section, they cut me in half, from front to back, like they were cleaving two sides of beef. It was butchery, not surgery. The scar still runs from the front all the way around to the base of my spine and, even though I had to go back six months later and go through surgery again, I still have physical problems as the result of it.

But they took the baby, and it seemed like an eternity before I finally heard him cry. I felt that something was wrong, because they had been checking the heartbeat every two or three minutes. I think they could tell that the baby was smothering. They had this table all prepared, where they took him and began to run tubes into him and suck on the tubes. I guess they were trying to clean him up and get him to breathe all at the same time. I waited and waited to hear that baby make a sound. He didn't, and I thought sure he was dead. But after about three minutes, I finally heard him cry.

I remember thinking *Oh, wow! It'll be okay now. I've finally got something to live for. I'm gonna get me a job, and I'm gonna straighten up and quit using drugs and everything's gonna be just great!*

All the while they were working on him, they were also working on me. I had 350 stitches when they finally got me sewed up. The doctor came around to the side of the bed, and I said, "Well, what did I have?"

I'll never forget his answer as long as I live. He just looked down at me over the top of that mask for a moment, and then he said, "Well, for right now, it's a boy."

I thought, *For right now? What does he mean? Is he out of his head or something? Either it's a boy, or it's a girl.*

After they finished with me, they wheeled me into the recovery room. I lay there for a couple of hours, and finally I got to the point where I wanted to see the baby. Finally the doctor came in. He stood there beside my bed and said, "Your little boy's very sick. He has something called acute respiratory syndrome. It's the same thing that killed President Kennedy's little boy. His body's full of mucus. He's drowning in his own fluids." Then he went into the corridor and told Claudine and Sharon, "Her baby's dying because of all the dope she has taken."

Claudine was all over that doctor like an enraged mother hen. "You idiot!" she screamed. "Are you out of your head? She hasn't taken any dope. If there's anything wrong with that baby, it's your fault for not taking care of her right."

The doctor just walked away. He had told her the truth and there wasn't anything more he could say. I didn't hear what he told her, but I heard Claudine and Sharon go to pieces, and I thought, *Oh, my God! My baby! He must be dead!*

The doctor came back into the room, and they were right behind him. He sat down on the edge of my bed and said, "Lu, you can have other children, you know. I'm sorry, but I don't think your baby's going to make it through the night. If by some small chance he should make it, there's a remote possibility that he might lead a normal, healthy life. I could fill you full of false hope, and I could lie to you, but I have to tell you the truth. I just don't think he'll make it through the night." Then he got up and walked out of the room.

Claudine just came apart. I had never told her I was into dope or any of the other things I was mixed up in. All through my life, whenever I needed help, Claudine had been there,and she wasn't about to leave me now. Neither one of them had eaten since the night before, so Sharon finally suggested that they go down and get some coffee, and they left me alone in the room.

By that time I was in a daze—just numb all over. I couldn't believe what the doctor had told me. I felt like it was all a dream. For a long time I lay there, just staring at the ceiling and not making a sound, but inside myself I was screaming. And finally the screaming turned into a kind of ranting and raving at God.

"Look!" I said, "I've always believed in You, God. I've gotten down. I got messed up with the wrong people, and I got into all the wrong things. I never took the time to get close to You, but I believe You're out there, somewhere. I know I've messed up my life and maybe it's too late for me. Maybe I'm going to hell, but what have You got against my baby? Why are You going to let him die? He hasn't been here long enough to do anything wrong!"

For the first time in my life, I felt like I was up against something I couldn't handle, and *I was scared silly!* I hurt terribly from all the butchering they'd done on me, but inside I hurt much worse with agony for my poor baby. I felt so helpless, so angry, and so terrified all at the same time. There wasn't anything else I could do, so I just lay there and bargained with God.

"If You're real, if You can hear me, and if You love me like they said You do, if You'll just let my baby live, then I'll do anything You say. I'll go where You want me to go and do what You want me to do. I'll get off dope, and I'll quit messin' around, and I'll not do anything except what You tell me to do." I said it over and over, only now I was saying it out loud.

I was in a room by myself because, generally, they do not put a mother whose baby has died in with mothers whose babies are all right. All of a sudden, I started to shake. Hard. All over. I shook so hard the whole bed shook, and I just kept on shaking. I couldn't cry or call out. All I did was lie there and shake.

It seemed that the shaking went on for hours. I couldn't remember the last time I had really prayed, probably it had been when I was still a kid back there at the Home, but I did remember one thing. It happened when I was still working for the clubs.

I awoke one afternoon and when I got up and looked out, it was one of the most beautiful days I could remember. A crisp, clear fall day, with everything washed and sparkling after a rain. My head wasn't buzzy, and I felt real good. Up, for a change, instead of down and icky like I usually felt when I woke up. I remembered standing at the window and thinking back to the days like that at the Home—running and jumping in piles of leaves, holiday times, good, clean fun.

Suddenly, I was sick of the clubs and of everything I was involved in. "Oh, God," I had said, "I want to get out of all this!"

It wasn't really a prayer, not consciously at least, but God must have heard it anyway because, two days later, along had come the telephone call about "Hee Haw."

If God had answered me then, I reasoned, if He had really been listening and had granted my prayer when I didn't even know I was praying, then surely He would do something for my baby now.

I was still arguing it all out in my mind, when Sharon walked in. "What're you talking about?" she asked.

"Oh, Sharon," I said, grabbing for her hand, "I'm so glad you're here! I'm so terribly afraid!"

She parked herself on the bed next to me and stayed with me all the way. When they came in and told her visiting hours were over, she simply refused to leave. Next morning, Claudine came back too, and the two of them hardly left my side all the while I was in the hospital.

While we were still in the operating room after the baby was born, I heard the doctor say, "Get Kraft on the phone." He was head pediatrician at Children's Medical Center. "We're sending your baby over there, because we don't have the equipment here to take care of him," the doctor said. "It's the only chance he has."

I hadn't even seen my baby, but my room was right across from the elevator, and when they brought the incubator out, I caught a glimpse of him while they waited for the elevator. Just a tiny, bloody little thing with tubes and needles sticking out all over him. Again, I felt this awful, clutching fear and again I started shaking.

A couple of hours later, in came a tall, silver-haired man. He was soft spoken, with kindly brown eyes. He sat down on the edge of my bed and took my hand in his. "I'm Doctor Kraft," he said, "and I've come to tell you about your baby. We're doing everything for him that we know how to do," he went on, "but he's a very sick little boy. I'll do everything I can, but only God can heal him."

Well I stayed in the hospital for eight days. Eight days that I didn't get to see my baby. Eight days that I was miserable. I just wanted to die. I called over there several times a day. "This is Miss Roman. Can you please tell me how my baby is?"

"He's in intensive care. He's being monitored very closely. He lost a couple of ounces today. I'm sorry. But he seems to be holding his own."

Then a couple of hours later, it was the same thing all over again. Sharon went over to Children's Hospital every day and took Polaroid pictures of him and brought them back to me. I just wanted to die. They had a needle stuck in his head with a little paper-cup-type cap over it. His arms were pinned down to his sides, and he was black and blue all over from the tests they had done on him. They checked him for diabetes, for jaundice, brain damage—everything. Before she would bring the pictures back to me, Sharon would go out and buy little presents—fruit baskets, hand lotion, cologne—things to try and cheer me up.

When I got out of the hospital, I got into Sharon's car and sat on a big pillow. I wouldn't go home until she took me over to that other hospital to see my baby. By this time he had progressed to where they had taken him out of the intensive-care unit and put him in a special-attention ward where they just monitored him. He still had the needles in his head, but he was unhooked from all the heart machines and other apparatus he'd been hooked up to.

When I first saw my baby, I hurt so badly for him I just broke down and cried. There was this big ward with six beds in it, and my little boy was lying there in the middle of a regular hospital bed with the sides pulled up on it. He was so tiny and so battered looking, I just wanted to die. In spite of the way they'd almost cut me in half, they still had taken him with forceps, and he had one black eye.

I sat there beside his bed, and I just shook all over and cried and cried. Finally I was told, "You'll have to go home now, Miss Roman." They wouldn't let me stay overnight, but I was right back there again as soon as they'd let me in the next morning.

Two or three days later, I had just gone home to get some rest when they called me on the phone and said, "Miss Roman, there's been a change in your baby's condition. You had better come over here."

When I got there, Dr. Kraft had been called off on another case, and this younger man was there to meet me. I can remember thinking, *What's wrong with you? Aren't you human? You're standing there fixing to tell me my baby's dying or something, and you don't even look concerned!*

We went up the elevator and down the hall to the same room, and he was saying, "I've been trying to think of what I could say to you, but I don't know what to say. I don't understand what's happened, but I've just done a thorough examination of your baby. He's been a very sick little boy, but I'm sorry, I can't find a thing wrong with him."

At first I didn't understand at all what he was saying, but by this time we were in the room, and there was my baby, lying in the middle of that big bed, just cooing away like there'd never been anything wrong with him. I watched them take the needle out of his head and unfasten his little hands. Then they dressed him in the little outfit I'd brought to the hospital with me, and they laid him in my arms.

"You . . . you mean he's all right?" I asked.

"That's right!" the doctor said. "They told me this baby was dying, but it looks to me like he just walked in here and said, 'Feed me; I'm hungry. Change me; I'm wet.' "

I carried him down to Sharon's car, and the first thing we did was drive straight to Claudine's.

All the while I was pregnant, she had ranted at me for going through with it. "What do you want a baby for, anyway?" she'd say. "You can't expect to bring up a young'un in the kind of life you're living."

She actually knew very little about the kind of life I was living. She knew about the go-go dancing because there was no way to avoid that with my face plastered all over the newspaper ads. But she didn't know about the dope or any of the rest of it. And all the while I was being dragged in and out of court, including the times she put up my bail, she simply refused to believe any of it was true. "They're lying, Louise," she'd say. "None of what they're saying about you is true. It's a frame-up."

Well, she didn't want me to have the baby, but you should have heard her when she saw him. "Oh, look at my baby," she cooed, taking him out of my arms. "Oh, what did they do to my baby?" as she gently touched the bruise that still showed around his eye. "My baby!" He was that the moment she saw him, and he still is.

We got back to the apartment finally, and Sharon took over. I had never even been around a small baby before, and I had no idea what he needed or how to take care of him. But Sharon knew. It was Sharon who fixed the formula and changed the diapers and came home in time for the 2:00 A.M. feeding.

I was still so weak I could hardly move. I was anemic, and I had lost a lot of blood in the hospital. In addition to that, I was so badly cut up that it took almost six months until I could sit down properly without scooching over on one side.

I took my baby home, and I went right back to what I had been doing. I started selling the dope again to buy our food and pay our rent, and I started hitting speed again almost immediately.

I had named my baby Damon Erik. He was well now, so I took all those promises I had made to God and pushed them out of my mind.

12

God Will Take Care of It

My lovely house was gone. My beautiful cars were gone. The man I had taken as my lover was gone, and all those people I had thought were my friends were gone, too. When the money and the dope and the food gave out, when I couldn't pay the rent on the house so they'd have a place to crash, they just disappeared one by one and left me alone.

One of the musicians I had known at the clubs was staying with us. I had run into him in the market one day and found out he was "between jobs" and didn't have a place to stay, so I invited him to come in with us until he found something. Danny wasn't into hard drugs, but he smoked pot, so we used to let him help us bag up the stuff we were selling. With all the freakies and dopies living there in the area around us, we felt a lot better having him in the apartment with us.

One night Danny and I were bagging up some speed when Sharon left for work. A couple of minutes later, there came a knock on the door. We thought it was Sharon coming back for something, but when Danny opened the door, here they were again—the narcotics squad, ten of 'em. They were going to make a really big deal of it. A regular front-page kind of raid. They had grabbed Sharon as she went to get into her car and had dragged her back in with them.

So here were Sharon and Danny and me, and they got all three of us for possession of dangerous drugs: marijuana, LSD, pills, a little dab of everything else and a bundle—a whole bundle—of speed.

I didn't know it then, but even when I had forgotten all about God and had reneged on my promises to Him, He was still watching out for me. Here they were, about to drag all three of us off to jail, and there I was with my baby on my knee! They had been there only ten minutes when there came another knock on the door. It was Polly, a younger girl who sometimes looked after Damon for me. She didn't know anything about the drugs and had just dropped in to pick up a sweater she had left, but right away they wanted to grab her and take her to jail, too.

"Look here!" I told them, "You keep your filthy hands off her. She's just my baby sitter, and she doesn't know a thing about all this!" They let her go and they let her take Damon with her, so all the while I was in jail, she and her mother took care of him.

One of Sharon's bosses came down and bailed her out right away so she could go to work that night, but Danny stayed there for almost two months. He didn't have anyone but his mother to bail him out, and it took her that long to raise the money.

And once again it was Claudine who saved my neck. She had a piece of property out in the country where she had thought about retiring someday. She put the deed to it on the line so they finally let me out.

When I got out of that place, I hadn't had a hit of speed for three and a half days, and I was really twitchy. I was starting to come off it cold and every bone in my body felt like somebody was banging on it with a sledgehammer. My head buzzed, my throat felt dry, and all I could think about was getting a hit.

Claudine took me over to the apartment, and then she went home. I raced up the stairs and rushed into the bathroom, but everything had been cleaned out this time—everything. There wasn't even an aspirin tablet in the whole place.

I knew I had things to think about. I had to make arrangements for the baby. I had to settle what I was going to do about the apartment and get in touch with my contacts, but right then all I could think about was that hit of speed.

I knew I was going to jail this time. The first case hadn't been settled yet. It was still dragging on in the courts, and now I had this one, too. The lawyer even told me, "I'm sorry, but there isn't a thing I can do. You're going to jail."

Sharon had a friend who was a doctor, and we had it fixed with him that we could go over there if we needed to and get a prescription. So I headed over there because, by this time, I was really shaking and hurting all over. Polly still had the baby, and I knew he was all right with her until I came for him, so I got a ride and went over to this doctor's office.

I walked through the door of that building and literally ran right into Patty's little sister. Diane had stayed with us a couple of times when we had the apartment together, but she didn't even look like the same girl. She was so neat and so shiny, even her face had a shininess about it, and the only word I could think of was *square*.

"Louise!" she screamed, "I've been praying I'd find you somehow. What are you doing here?" And before I could answer, she started asking a million questions: where was I living? what was I doing? did I know Patty had moved? and on and on and on. And all the while I was thinking, *My gawd I've gotta get away from her before I go to pieces and die right here on this spot.*

Finally I broke in. "Look, Diane," I said, "I'm very, very sick, and I've got an appointment with the doctor, and I'm late already. I'm sorry, but I've gotta go. Call me sometime, huh?" and I started for the elevator.

"What's your number?" she yelled as the elevator door was closing, and I blurted it out.

Then I thought, *You fool! You crazy fool! You've given your phone number to the squarest person you've seen in years, and if she finds out what you're doing, that's sure bust number three!* I went on up and got my "prescription," and pretty soon I forgot about Diane.

That afternoon I was spaced out on the rug of my apartment, lying there just drifting and listening to the radio, when the phone rang. "Louise? This is Diane. I know you're in trouble, Lu. I've been reading about it in the paper, and I've been praying that I'd run into you or find you somewhere. The Lord answered that prayer when I saw you today. I want to help, Lu. I want very much to help. I love you, and I'd like to do what I can."

I love you. Hmmm. I couldn't remember ever hearing any other woman ever saying that to me before. Not even Claudine or my mother. I'm sure they did love me in their own way, but they just didn't put it into words.

Once more, all I could think about was getting away from that chatter, so I said all right and gave her my address. Somewhere in the back of my fog-filled brain the idea may have been floating around that perhaps Diane could take care of the baby if I was sentenced and had to go to jail.

That evening, they came—Diane and her older brother. I knew they had come to talk, but I didn't know what we could possibly talk about, so I dug up everything I could to keep busy. I cleaned up the kitchen while Diane stood there and yakked to me, then I bathed the baby and fed him and put him to bed. Finally I just ran out of things to do, so I sat down and tried to think of something to say.

"Everything must be going all right for you," I said. "You look happy and on top of the world."

"Oh, Louise, I am happy," she said, "and everything is just wonderful with me. I found Jesus! I've given my life to Him, and everything has just changed completely."

I said, "Uh . . . oh, yeah."

Well she started in then and told me how it all happened. I had heard from Patty every once in a while so I knew how things were with her. After I got fired from the telephone company, she had been transferred to another area. Since then, she had married, and now she had three children.

But their father's condition had worsened and before he died, he called all the family together and made them promise that they would get back into church. "He said he wanted us to get right with God," Diane said.

Giving their lives to Jesus had just changed everything, Diane insisted. "I know He could help you, too," she said once, but I made no comment, and she didn't press the point.

Then we got around to talking about old times. About all the things we could think of—the funny things and the serious things, the heartaches and the beatings—all the things we both could remember about the Home. And every time I got off on how rough some of the housemothers had been to Patty and her little brother, Diane would burst out with, "But it doesn't matter now, Louise. Jesus has just changed all that and taken away all the hurt."

After a while I started to cry, and I said, "Diane, do you have any idea what I have done with my life? You look so happy, so . . . so clean and shining, and I'm so miserable I could die. Do you realize what I've done? I've tried everything, Diane. Everything. I've tried money and men and sex and drugs. I even tried show business, and I made it, too. I was really going great on 'Hee Haw,' but I blew it. I had everything I've ever wanted. A beautiful house, a big Continental, money, friends, everything money could buy, but I let it all just slip away. I don't have any money. I'm hooked on dope. I have a baby, and I'm not married, and I'll probably have to go to jail. You keep saying that Jesus changed everything around in your life. Well, I guess I need Jesus or something a whole lot more than you did."

Diane hit the floor screaming. She jumped straight up off the couch yelling, *"Praise the Lord, Louise!* That's why we're here!"

I'd never heard anything like that before. It scared me so bad, I nearly went right out the back door. You start screaming at somebody who's had a big old hit of drugs, and they'll hang right off the ceiling. Maybe you think the reason all those hippies and freakies speak so quietly is because they're soft and gentle people. Don't you believe it! They talk softly because they can't stand noise.

For the next few minutes I just sat there trying to get back down and finally I said, "What did you say?" And she said it again, "Praise God, Louise, that's why we're here."

So I sat there and listened to them tell me all about how Jesus had changed their lives. They were stunned by their father's dying wish that they get right with God, but they went back to church as he had asked them to do and before long they had all been saved. I sat there, just listening and letting the tears run down my face.

There was something so sweet and precious and good about all that they were saying. Not at all like the sermons they used to yell at us at the Home. Nothing about punishment or hell or damnation. Just goodness and gentleness . . . and love.

They left after a while, but several days later Diane said, "There's some place that I want to take you. Some place where you can really get help. I'll bring someone to stay with the baby one night, and I want you to go with me."

By that time I would have gone anywhere with anybody if I thought it would help, so I said okay and they left.

A couple of days later, she came again, and this time she brought her friend Paula and five big sacks of groceries. The two of them just took over. Sharon had moved in with another one of her boyfriends, and there was no one with me in the apartment. For several months Diane and Paula took care of me. They paid my rent, bought my groceries, and even bought baby food, diapers, and clothes for my baby.

I wondered how they did it, just two single girls working in regular jobs—nothing spectacular or out of the ordinary as far as salary was concerned—taking over the full load for my baby and me. One day when I said something about it, Diane said, "I can't see where it has hurt us in any way, Louise. We're not going hungry, and we're not doing without anything we need."

Then again Diane said she wanted to take me someplace. "It's the Beverly Hills Baptist Church right here in Dallas," she said, "and I want you to go there with me."

"Baptist!" I shrieked. "The people out at the Home were Baptist. I shouldn't think anyone in your family would ever look at a Baptist again."

"These people are different," she said. "They aren't anything like the people at the Home. I really want you to come with me, Louise," she said.

"Okay," I said, "I promised, so I'll go with you—one time."

Paula gave me her credit card for a large department store and told me to go down there the next day and get myself "something decent to wear to church." I got a long dark dress with long sleeves to cover up the needle marks in my arms. Next Sunday night, Diane and Paula came, and away we all went to church, taking the baby with us.

"My gawd," I said to Diane as we got out of the car, "they must be having bingo or something!" There were cars parked all over the parking lot and for blocks around on every side street. Finally we found a place in a supermarket lot and walked back. "It seems kind of funny, going to church again," I said. "I haven't been to church since I left the Home."

I don't know what I expected, but this place wasn't anything like it. First of all, it was packed. There was just enough room for us to squeeze into one of the pews near the back. We slid into one of those, right next to the aisle, and it looked as if every other bit of space in that whole place was filled. There were even people sitting on the floor up in front and standing against the walls on both sides.

I was glad we were way in the back, close to the door. That way, I thought, if things started getting too heavy I could pretend I had to take care of Damon and get out.

A man was playing the organ when we came in and then a tall, silver-haired man came out onto the platform. There was no signal of any kind—no one said, "Let's turn to hymn so and so"—but pretty soon everyone just started singing something called "He Is Lord." I listened for a couple of minutes, and then I started breaking out in goose bumps all over. There was an older man and his wife sitting right in front of me, and they put their hands up in the air and went right on singing, "He is Lord." I thought what *is* it? These people must be a bunch of Holy Rollers in here. So I dug Diane in the ribs and said, "You did say this was a *Baptist* church, didn't you?" And she said, "Yes," with a wide, silly grin and went right on singing.

I looked around some more and now it wasn't just one or two, it was all over the place. They all had their hands up in the air, and they were still singing. They were into something called "Allelujah," singing it in a kind of chant. It was so beautiful, it made me cry. Those hands were still up in the air, so I got into Diane's ribs again and said, "Are you *sure* this is a Baptist church?" and she said, "I'm a member," so I sat down and kept quiet. But I also kept one eye on the door.

The singing had never been anything like that at the Home. Even the different groups who came out there from time to time had never affected me like this. The music seemed to set up a vibration that went through and through me, and I liked the way it made me feel.

Then the pastor got up and gave the message, but I couldn't follow very much of what he said because I'd had a hit of speed before I came over there to bolster myself up, and by now I was so wired, I felt paranoid. I was afraid, scared of what might happen, scared of the people, scared of what I might do and how I might embarrass Diane.

They started singing again, and I thought it must be time for the benediction. I looked up and there was that pastor, walking down the steps of the platform and coming straight down the aisle. It was a long stretch of red carpet all the way from the platform to the door we had come in by, and he was walking along it with his head down and his eyes focused on the carpet. I thought, "Oh, good Lord, he's coming after me!"

I had never seen anybody go down and get somebody like that before, but I just knew he was coming for me and that's just exactly what he did. I threw a quick glance at Diane, and she was shaking her head, no! no! I heard her whisper, "Not yet. Oh, please, not yet. This is her first time. You'll scare her away," but he kept right on coming.

He stopped right there in the aisle right next to where I was sitting. He took hold of both of my hands and his look went right through me. He said, "I know who you are, and I wouldn't embarrass you for anything in the world." Oh sure! Right after he had just walked all the way from the front of that church and every eye in the place had turned and followed him! "I don't want to embarrass you," he said, "but could I introduce you to my church?"

I don't remember saying yes. I don't remember saying anything at all, but the next thing I knew, he had hold of my hand, and I was following him down that aisle—all the way to the front of the church! My knees were shaking, and I was trembling all over. All I could think of was, *How do I get out of here?*

But the pastor was saying, "How many of you people watch television?" and every hand went up. Then he said, "How many of you watch 'Hee Haw'?" and every hand seemed to go up again. "I want you to meet LuLu," he said and all over the place people started clapping and getting to their feet. It was a standing ovation. I had never experienced anything like that. They started crowding in around me, and I couldn't see through the people. They started touching—my hands, my arms, my back, shoulders, and head. I thought, *Are they going to get my clothes?* I'd seen that done in a couple of rock places, and suddenly I was scared again.

But this was different. There was a kind of buzzing, and then I realized all these people were saying something. "I love you, LuLu. God bless you, LuLu. We're praying for you, dear. I love you. I love you. I love you."

Somewhere out of the haze of the speed I had taken, I can remember thinking, I paid money to hear someone say "I love you," and here are all these people I've never seen before, and they're saying "I love you" and it's free! They don't want anything from me. They're just saying they love me, and once more I started to cry. I didn't have any idea of what a sweet spirit was. I'd never heard of a conviction. I only knew that something strange was going on around me and for the first time, I felt that it was real. But it scared me, and all I could think about was getting out.

When we did get out of there and back into the car again, I just sat there. Diane asked something like, "How'd you like my church?" but I just mumbled. When they let me out in front of the apartment she said, "We'll pick you up again next Wednesday night."

I didn't answer her, but inside I was thinking, *No way! Over my dead body!* But on Wednesday night, they came again, and we went back—again and again and again—every time the door was open. And every time I went back, I noticed things I hadn't seen before.

There was the time I got to looking around, and it seemed that everyone in the place was lit up with that silly grin that Jesus gives you. I thought, *They must have problems. I know they have problems!* But I couldn't see one unhappy face in the whole place. I noticed how whole families came there together, even little babies and very old people. And everyone seemed so much at home. Children got up from their pews and went to the bathroom by themselves just as they would in their own homes, and some folks took off their shoes when they wanted to.

But it was the singing that got to me. It was so harmonious and so beautiful. Sometimes it would be fast and lively, filling you full of pep and enthusiasm, and sometimes it was so hushed and quieting it made you feel that everyone was just talking to God out of the depths of his own spirit.

I knew they called this church *charismatic,* but I wasn't sure just what that meant. I didn't want to ask Diane, because I was beginning to like what I felt when I went there, and I didn't want her to tell me anything that would upset that feeling. So I just let it drift along like everything else in my life was drifting.

Going to church had set up a schism within me. I felt like two people warring against each other. Part of me knew I should get out and get a job, get off drugs, pull myself together, and get my life straightened out. I had promised God I would do that if He'd heal my baby. But the other part of me felt dragged down and despairing. I didn't know how to do anything decent to make a living except be a telephone operator, and they weren't likely to take me back again. Besides, what would I do with the baby?

Sharon had moved out after we were arrested. We kept in touch, and she had brought me money a couple of times, but she was living in another apartment now, "keeping house" for another one of her "friends."

Claudine couldn't take him even though she'd like nothing better. She was still working at the hotel. I could leave him with Polly, but I didn't want to give my baby over to someone else to raise.

All these things kept buzzing around in my head and pretty soon I'd be back in the bathroom, giving myself that hit of speed I still thought I needed.

Then one night we went to church again, and I found out a little bit more about what that word *charismatic* meant.

Diane and I were sitting on the side aisle this time, more toward the middle of the church. The pastor had started his message when suddenly a man hurried up to the platform from way in the back and said something to one of the associate pastors who was sitting up there, and they both went to the back of the church. I turned around to look, but it was solid people again, and I couldn't see through them.

The pastor stopped himself right in the middle of a sentence and explained. "I see one of our members is having a little problem," he said, "and Brother William is anointing with oil, so let's all praise the Lord."

There they went again with that "Allelujah" thing and this time it sent a tingly feeling up my spine and made the hair stand up on the back of my neck. All around me, people were standing with their hands up in the air, singing "Al-le-lu-jah, Al-le-lu-jah" over and over, and other people seemed to be singing a sort of descant to it like an eight or more part song. It all blended together in an unearthly, heavenly kind of sound, different from anything I had ever heard, until it seemed to reverberate through and through that whole building and everybody in it.

Once, I had gotten hold of an electric wire that was lying in some water, and I now felt that tingling sensation going through my whole body. What were they doing, I wondered. Was this exorcism? Were they trying to cast out devils?

Then I remembered something else. I had gone to the dentist to have my teeth cleaned, and as I was leaving, the hygienist was working with a probe-like instrument that was giving off a high-frequency sound like I had heard in the studios. I asked what she was doing, and she said, "I'm using this ultrasonic instrument to clean this denture. In other words, I'm cleaning it with sound."

"How does it work?" I asked.

"I'm not sure," she said, "but I think it has something to do with vibration."

I had heard the pot-smoking people who had hung out around my place talking about vibrations. Sometimes when we were way down about something, we'd all hold hands and sit cross-legged on the floor and chant "to raise the vibes," as it was called. And it worked, because, after a few minutes, we all felt like we'd been lifted out of the mood that was swallowing us.

Is that what these people were doing? Raising the vibes? Using the music to cleanse people with sound? Whether that's what they intended to do or not, it certainly worked, too, because after a few minutes of that "Allelujah" music, I felt like I was halfway to heaven.

Another thing that got to me was the love of all those people. "Hello, LuLu," they'd say. "It's so good to have you back." "I'm glad to see you again." "We're praying for you." Things like that, they'd say, and always there was the hug or the handshake or the warm, gentle touch that made me know they meant it.

It was on a Wednesday night, a little more than a month from the first time I went there. Diane and I were sitting way up in the back again; the choir was singing; people were going up to the platform and others were taking hold of their hands or hugging them, and there was a sweet, loving spirit in the place like I'd never felt before.

I didn't know what it meant to be under conviction, but the tears were running down my face, and I knew that I wanted whatever it was that those people had more than anything I'd ever wanted in my life.

I couldn't bring myself to stand on my feet and walk down that aisle because of some remnant of my feeling about all that still clung to me from the Home. But I leaned over and poked Diane, and between sobs, I said to her, "I've got to talk to that man."

"Praise God!" Diane said out loud. Then *she* walked down the aisle, all the way to the platform, and she said to the pastor, "Brother Howard, she wants to talk."

After the service was over, Diane took me to his study, and before long, he came in. Tall, silver haired, with those blue, blue eyes that looked right through you—he just smiled and sat down behind his desk and didn't say anything. I didn't give him a chance.

As soon as he sat down, I jumped up and said, "Let me tell you how it's gonna be, okay, mister?" Then I began telling him everything I wasn't gonna give up if I got saved. It would have been hysterical on television, but he didn't say a word. He just sat there and let me rave on.

"I ain't never gonna give up marijuana," I said, "because they don't make anything better."

"God didn't tell me to tell you not to smoke marijuana," he said.

Oh, wow! I thought. This man is smoking marijuana! But before I had a chance to pursue that, he stuck his finger in the middle of my nose and said, "God will take care of that!" It sounded like thunder.

I said, "Yeah, man." Then I said, "I've got a baby, and I'm not married."

"God will take care of that."

I didn't tell him about the dope, but later I found out he had already seen the needle marks on my arms. "I've got three or four boyfriends, and they're goodies, and I'm not gonna give them up either," I said.

"God will take care of that."

"Well," I said, "I'm on my way to jail!"

"God will take care of that, too."

To everything I said, I got the same answer, "God will take care of that."

Then that old spirit of rebellion rose up inside me, and I thought, *Can't that fool say anything except "God will take care of that?" Who does he think he is, anyway—telling me what God's gonna do?*

I was mad, and I let him know it, because I literally cussed him out. Then I sat down on the couch and told him my whole life story—every vile and filthy thing I could think of—and when I got all through, I just fell over on the couch and cried and cried.

And he just sat there and didn't say a word.

Finally, I sat up and said, "Now you just tell me how you think God's gonna forgive me for all of that!"

I was convinced that I had gone too far. I had gone back on my promises to God, and I really believed He just wasn't interested in me anymore. Back at the Home, there hadn't been a great deal of emphasis placed on forgiveness.

The pastor stood up from behind his desk and came around to where I was sitting. Then he sat down on the floor in front of the couch. "Come here," he said, patting a place on the carpeting next to him, so I got up and sat down on the floor beside him.

Then very simply, like he might tell it to a four-year-old, he told me the story of Jesus—not religion, not doctrine, not theology—just the story of the man called Jesus: how He came into this world to save people from their sins; how He went to Calvary and shed His blood and died on the cross out of love for people like me; how He didn't want me to be like this, full of dope, lonely, hurt, rejected and burdened with guilt.

"Now," the pastor said, "do you want to go on carrying all that stuff around that you've been telling me about, or would you just like to lay it down at the foot of the Cross?"

I didn't have any idea what that meant. I just knew that I wanted to look like all those people looked out there in that church. I wanted to be able to smile and have it come from my heart. I knew I had to have peace of mind, and if this was the way to get it, then let's go ahead.

So we knelt right there on the floor—Pastor Howard Conatser and I. We said a very simple sinners' prayer, and I gave my heart to Jesus. And when I got up again, I felt lighter. I felt like a burden had been lifted from me, and I was singing inside. I rolled down the window of Diane's car, and all the way home I kept shouting, "Praise the Lord! Praise the Lord!"

"That's how I felt, too," Diane said.

"And now everything's gonna be all right in my life, isn't it?" I said. "Everything's just gonna be hunky-dory."

"We-ell, I wouldn't say that," she smiled. "You see, the devil doesn't let go that easily. When we take a firm stand for Jesus, the devil usually throws all kinds of problems and temptations in our way to see if we really mean it."

Oh! She was so right! And what she didn't tell me was how those problems sneak up on you when you're the most vulnerable and the least prepared for them.

But the next day I thought I had really made progress. It was still morning, and I was up and had my breakfast, had bathed the baby, and was cleaning up the place. Suddenly, I felt like I wanted to get rid of all that hippy, freaky junk I had around the place. I had torn down posters, was throwing out incense, and was thinking about how to get rid of the strobe lights and the psychedelic garbage when my next-door neighbor walked in.

We sat there, yakked for a while, and had a couple of Cokes when finally she said, "What's wrong with you? You sure act different. You haven't said a single cussword all morning!"

I sat there for a minute trying to think of how to tell her, and then I just blurted it out. "There isn't anything wrong. I gave my life to Jesus. I got saved!"

It blew her mind! I had just done to her what Diane once did to me, and she couldn't handle it. I had just screamed, "I got saved!" at a very stoned young lady. She shook her head a couple of times as though her ears were ringing, then she got up and stared at me as if she wanted to ask, "Saved from what?" but she just opened the door very quietly and left. But God made His point with her, because, in time, she was one of the first ones He used me to bring into His precious Kingdom.

Later, I carried all that stuff out to the trash bin and was starting back up the stairs to the apartment when a movement under one of the steps caught my eye. I backed down the steps and went around to see what it was.

There, hanging in a corner of the step, was a big ugly-looking black- white- and yellow-striped caterpillar. It had fastened itself to the underneath side of the step and was hanging upside down. As I watched, it gave a jerk, and then I saw that it was actually splitting open. With each convulsion, the skin opened a little further along the back and rolled upward.

Patty's mother had told me that you couldn't see what it was that became a butterfly. It was a spark of life, invisible, like the human soul. Well, I was certainly seeing it now. Inside that caterpillar there was something shiny and pale green with little flecks of gold in it, and the caterpillar was taking off its coat so the green butterfly could fly free. Pretty smart, I thought. But why was it hanging upside down? Why didn't it just loosen the coat around the collar and shed it that way?

I kept an eye on it as I went up and down the steps with several loads. Then, when it appeared to have the outer skin rolled all the way up, I stopped and watched some more. What I thought was a green butterfly was actually a little silken bag that was gradually turning into a fuzzy brown cocoon, just like the one I had poked open at the Home the time Patty's mother tried to stop me.

Suddenly the caterpillar just dropped away, skin, head, and all and left the fuzzy brown bag hanging there. Okay! So something inside it was going to turn into a butterfly, but how could it? What was directing the operation, now that the head was gone?

Then a whole jumble of thoughts flew through my mind—being born again, butterflies as a symbol of the Spirit, and being a new creature in Christ. "Behold I make all things new!"

Suddenly, it all came together in a flood of realization and joy. Jesus didn't need my thoughts or ideas or opinions. All my concepts about people, about the world, and even about religion had been formed out of my experiences while I was groveling in the dirt. My ideas were of the earth—earthy. I could just toss them all out with the rest of the trash I'd been hauling out all morning.

What did I *really* know about Jesus and the realm of the spirit anyway? Absolutely nothing. But it didn't matter, because *He* was in control. *He* had the blueprint for my life. He knew what He wanted me to become. All I had to do was get my bloated nothingness out of the way and let it happen.

Later that afternoon Sharon came with a new outfit she had bought for the baby. We sat and talked for a while, and when she said, "What have you been doing with yourself?" I just let it all run out.

I went on about how wonderful I felt, about the joy and peace and knowing, somehow, that it was all going to work out—now that I had given my life to Jesus.

"I knew something pretty big must have happened to you," she said. "You sure act different. You even look different. I've known you a long time, and I've never seen you look like this—so calm, quiet, and peaceful. And I've never heard you go this long without cussing, either."

She rubbed out her cigarette in the ashtray and got up to leave. But before she went, she came around the end of the table and gave me a big hug.

After she left, I sat there for quite a while sorting out my feelings. I felt sorry for her. I actually felt sorry for Sharon! And all the time I had known her, I had envied her. And another thing—I had *witnessed!* The pastor had talked about how I needed to share Jesus with others. Well, I had told the gal next door about giving my life to Jesus, and now I had told Sharon. The results weren't exactly what you could call earthshaking, but at least I had done my part.

And then it struck me—hard. I hadn't had a hit of speed for twenty-four whole hours! A whole day! And I hadn't even thought about it. I simply went off it cold—just like that—without one single pain or withdrawal symptom of any kind. I hadn't even realized it was happening, and I have never had a need for drugs again.

Diane and Paula were witnesses to my deliverance. They were around to see it happen. Praise God I have witnesses to God's deliverance!

13

You've Changed, Kiddo!

About six months after the baby was born, I had to go back into the hospital for repair of the butchery job that had been done on me, and while I was there, I really had an excellent chance to compare the B.C. and A.D. phases of my life.

First, there was my attitude toward the doctor who was responsible for carving me up. I still hated his guts, but not as vehemently and not in the same language as before.

Then there was the matter of faith—the "God will take care of it" affirmation of Brother Howard. I was still treading on very shaky ground where that one was concerned. It certainly seemed to work for him, but how could I be sure it would work for me. I knew I had been saved. I knew God had forgiven me for my sins. But deep down inside of me, I still felt that God had me on probation.

Then along came one of those "coincidences" that never seems to fit entirely into the pattern of mere happenstance.

Before I could go to the hospital, I had to find someone to take care of the baby. Polly was no longer available, and everyone else I knew was working. It had come right down to the wire as far as time was concerned, and I was just going to call an agency as a last resort when I went digging into an old purse, trying to find a pencil. As I turned it upside down and shook it, a slip of paper fell out.

"Ivy Edwards," it said. And there was a telephone number. Now just who . . . oh, yes! She was the lady my attorney had told me about.

"If ever you need someone to look after your baby, you can call this lady," he said when he wrote down her name and number. "Ivy's had nine kids of her own, and she takes care of children for a living. She's good. I know she's good, because she takes care of mine. She knows all about you, and she told me if ever you needed her, she'd take care of your baby free of charge."

Well, what do you do when you're completely out of money, and you're desperately in need of a baby sitter? Formerly, I would have bolstered my courage with a hit of speed, but this was A.D., and I turned to the Lord instead.

I know that A.D. means "anno Domini" for most people—"in the year of the Lord." But I've added a very personal meaning to it. A.D., for me, means "after Damon," the name of my firstborn son, and I might never have turned back toward God if I had never had him. It was when he was so sick in the hospital, that I asked for God's help to heal him, and even though I forgot about my bargain and slid right back into drugs again, still it was my first step toward salvation.

The helplessness and suffering of that little boy awakened the mother instinct and every other drug-deadened bit of decency within me and made me turn toward Someone bigger than I for help.

And now I turned to Him again. "Please, Jesus," I prayed, "give me the courage and the humility to ask for the help I need." Then I dialed the number and said, "This is LuLu Roman."

"Why, LuLu!" said this warm, friendly, motherly voice, "I've been asking the Lord when He was going to give me an opportunity to meet you."

Well, not only did she take care of Damon, but she insisted that I come to her home, too, when I got out of the hospital. She took care of both of us until I could be up on my feet again.

But it was while I was still in the hospital that I had a very good opportunity to look at what I had been and what I hoped I could become. It all came together when Diane and Paula were visiting me one day when two of my former dancer friends walked in.

I was looking at Paula, and she was looking toward the door, when suddenly her eyes opened to about three times their normal size and I heard her breath come in a long sssssssssss between her teeth. I turned over and looked, and there they were, two streetwalkers typecasted down to the last detail. Long, curly, bleached-blond hair, junky-looking jewelry—too much and too big—plunging necklines, piled on makeup, short, short skirts that barely covered their fannies, and high-heeled, red shoes.

"Hi, Lu," said Mamie between loud cracks of her gum, "wyinheck din ya tell us you were havin' an opening?"

"Yeah," laughed Zelda, "we'da sold tickets and bought out the whole place."

When I could get a word in, I introduced them to Diane and Paula. Diane could handle it. After all, she had been to our place quite a few times when Patty and I were rooming together. But poor little Paula had never seen anything like it in her life. She just scooted back her chair into a corner and almost melted into the woodwork, turning all shades of red at the conversation, but not saying a word. Paula had been raised by her grandparents—good, Christian people—and she had never been exposed to anyone like Mamie and Zelda.

Diane must have sensed how she felt, because in a few moments, she made some excuse, and the two of them left.

I guess I had never really understood what the word *coarse* meant before, but I saw it all very plainly now. These two gals were really very good hearted. Either one of them would have done anything they could to help me, or anyone else who needed a friend. But in looking at them, all I could think of was a circus poster. And I was surprised to discover that I actually felt embarrassed to hear them using words I had been using myself only a few short weeks before.

I didn't feel better than them; only relieved that I wasn't like them anymore. And I felt sorry, very sorry, that they weren't enjoying the same freedom from that kind of life that I was feeling. So when Mamie said, "You're changed, kiddo. You don't even look like the same person," I thought this was my opportunity to share with them.

"I'm *not* the same person," I told them. "All the old things have passed away, and I'm a new person. I've given my life to Jesus."

"You *what?*" Mamie screamed.

"Cheez!" said Zelda. "This kid's really freaked out. They musta given her a shot of morphine or something. Let's get outta here before she starts preachin'."

"No, wait," I started to say, "you don't understand . . . ." But they hurried out of the room.

They were the first, but they weren't the last ones. Everything I was and everything I wanted to be seemed to come together and clash in that hospital room. Even Claudine was shook up about it.

"Look," she said one day after she had met Brother Howard and some other people from the church, "I know this church experience means a lot to you, and I'll have to admit it's certainly changed you for the better, but I simply don't get all this Jesus talk, all this praying. Noboby—*nobody*—can be that holy!"

Well, I'd gone all through that, too, and Diane had never argued with me when I spouted off. So I just kept quiet and said, "God will take care of it," inwardly, to myself, so she couldn't hear.

Shortly before I went into the hospital, I had led a Jesus march through some of the main streets with folks from our church. I carried a big sign that said, I'M HIGH ON JESUS. I'VE BEEN SET FREE.

The newspaper splashed it all across the front pages. "HEE HAW'S" LULU KICKS THE DRUG HABIT, SAYS SHE'S HIGH ON JESUS. If anyone had missed the fact that I had been a dopie, they sure knew it now!

The people at church were all so kind and loving, and I didn't go anywhere much except there. But whenever I pulled into a filling station or went to the market or the doctor's office, little knots of people would gather to point and whisper and stare. For months and months, I felt like a creature from another planet. My former friends kept away, because I wasn't talking their language or doing their thing anymore, and the people I wanted to meet and be friends with rejected me as though I were some kind of monster.

The embarrassment and humiliation kept on while I was still in the hospital. I had to ask the nurses to keep my door closed, because I felt so awful when visitors who were walking along the hallway would stop to stare at me, then stand there whispering. And poor Claudine! I'm sure something inside of her died a little the day a thoughtless co-worker said, "Wow! That granddaughter of yours sure made the headlines, didn't she?" But she kept right on sticking up for me and telling herself that everything she read in the papers was all a pack of lies.

But there was something else that began to happen while I was still in the hospital, and with that, I came to see that perhaps the Lord could find a use for my life after all.

Diane and Paula came hurrying into my room one evening, and Diane was waving a letter all excitedly and saying, "Look, Lu, these people over at Lakeridge want you to come and give your testimony. Isn't that wonderful?"

"I dunno," I said. "That all depends. Where is Lakeridge and what is a testimony?"

"Lakeridge," she said, "is a new little spirit-filled Baptist church across town. They're asking you to come over and tell how you were saved. That's called 'giving your testimony.' "

"Oh," I said. "We-ell, I'll have to see about that. Will you help me write it?"

"Look, Lu," she said, "you don't write a testimony. You stand up and *tell* it. All you have to do is tell them about how you were raised at the Home and how you got off on the wrong foot when you got out of there and just got deeper and deeper into sin until the Lord let me run into you that day. And then you tell them about going to church and about giving your heart to Jesus right there in Brother Howard's study and how your life has changed since then. Now that's how you give your testimony, but I think we better practice a few times on yours, because I'm sure we're going to have to do some editing."

Remember, I was still in the hospital when all this was going on and suddenly another thought hit me.

"Did they send any money?" I asked. Paula and Diane were still paying my rent and buying my groceries, and the unemployment insurance I was still drawing from "Hee Haw" was the only income I had.

"Money," Diane said, "why would they send money?"

"Well, speakers usually get paid, don't they," I said, "and besides, we're gonna have to buy gas to drive up there, and I hafta have something to wear."

"It's different at churches," Diane said. "They usually take up a love offering, and the speaker's expenses are covered by that."

"What we ought to do," Paula suggested, "is set up a corporation or association if you're going to be doing very much of this kind of thing. Then you would be entitled to a salary and expenses out of that, and we could keep records for income-tax purposes."

You could depend upon Paula to keep things orderly, proper, and legal. She worked for a brokerage firm and knew all about business details. We might have been prophetic, or maybe it was just optimistic, but at any rate we formed a verbal association right on the spot. I put in the twenty dollars I still had left from that week's unemployment check, and Diane and Paula each put in ten dollars. We called ourselves "LuLu Roman Saved to Serve Incorporated," with me as president, Diane as vice president, and Paula as secretary-treasurer.

The invitation to speak at Lakeridge was set for a month ahead, and I felt sure I would be healed enough to go by then, so Paula wrote a letter of acceptance. And while I was recuperating, a few more invitations from other churches came in.

I went to Ivy's house directly from the hospital, and Diane came over in the evenings to help me with my testimony. Like she said, it needed some editing, but we didn't give it nearly enough. Maybe we should have written it, after all, and then I could have memorized it word for word. Instead, what we did was make out an outline of my life story. We put it on three-by-five cards, so I could lay those on the pulpit and use them as a guide to be sure I got in everything.

On the day we were supposed to go, it rained like the flood was starting all over again. I don't think the devil wanted me to go to that church. Paula couldn't go, so Diane and another friend of hers came to call for me. The rain was pouring down and the driving was very bad, so that when we got there, we were forty-five minutes late.

We went inside and looked around. There couldn't have been more than twenty-five or thirty people in the whole place. At first I was humiliated, but then the Lord impressed it upon me that if only one soul came to Jesus, the whole trip would be worth it.

I stood up there and did the very best I could, and when I was all through, the pastor came up and put his arm around me. "LuLu, honey," he said. "I hear you've been seeking."

Oh, wow! I thought. *What's his angle.* "Seeking what?" I asked.

"The Holy Spirit," he smiled, and I just froze. I was pretty sure of what was going to happen next, because I'd seen this several times at Beverly Hills Baptist Church. All I could think of was getting out of there. But there was no way I could get out.

"I want all the ladies to come up here and lay their hands on LuLu and pray for her," the pastor said, and up they came. They crowded in all around me—about eight or ten of them, I guess—and put their hands on my head, my shoulders, my arms. Then there came this chatter, and I knew they were praying in the spirit, but I just couldn't believe this was happening to me!

They went on for twenty minutes or so, and I was so embarrassed and humiliated that I just wanted to run away, but they went right on—and on and on and on. I was feeling weak, so I just closed my eyes and stood there, waiting for them to quit. Finally, I had a shocking revelation. *They weren't going to quit!* They were not going to stop until they had accomplished what they had set out to do—even if it took all night! I was so upset by that time that I just wanted to drop.

Finally, I just closed my eyes and prayed. *Lord, I'm really embarrassed. I can't fake it. I don't know how, and they won't stop until something happens. Father, if this is Your will and if it's my time, I will receive it."*

Then, suddenly, I heard myself talking in a heavenly language, louder than all the rest. I got so drunk in the Spirit, that it took

Diane, another lady, and two men to get me out of the place.

After I had calmed down again, I realized that I had spent ten years of my life, wasting away on drugs, spending all my time and money trying to get myself high and, praise God, *I had never been that high in all those years!*

Today, I'm still high on Jesus. I didn't spend one penny to get that way, and I can't ever go to jail for it either. This is the kind of "high" that never lets you down. It brings peace and joy with it and a wonderful sense of knowing that everything's all right. It comes from knowing Jesus and having Him in my heart. Jesus has set me free to reach a new and beautiful height in His precious love and grace.

14

The Scars on My Heart Prove It

The "LuLu Roman Saved to Serve" organization went on for about a year and a half, muddling into one problem after another and the three of us blaming each other. We made all kinds of mistakes. We got into trouble over money and taxes and squabbled among ourselves. We took advice from people who meant well, but simply didn't have the kind of experience we needed. The only thing that went right was that I was polishing my talk with every speaking engagement, and somewhere along the line, the Lord started using it to move people toward Him.

Finally, I think He got tired of seeing us bickering among ourselves, wasting the time that could be used more profitably for Him, so He arranged another one of those "coincidences."

For some time, people in our own church and in other churches where I went to speak had been telling us about Mark Carter. Whenever we ran into some kind of business problem, they'd say, "You ought to get in touch with Mark Carter," or "Mark Carter could show you how to straighten out your affairs." When I finally decided that we simply *had* to look him up, the Lord practically put him in my lap.

Brother Howard Conatser, his secretary, and I were having lunch in a restaurant one day when there came a slender, dark-haired, very pleasant man to our table. "I'm Mark Carter," he said, holding out his hand, and I nearly flipped! I'd been hearing about him for months, and now the Lord had brought him right to me!

Well, Mark always says he's seen a lot of strange reactions when people meet him for the first time, but I'm the only one who ever broke right down and cried! I actually did! I held out my hand to him with tears streaming down my cheeks and said, "I-I'm so g-glad to m-meet you," between sobs.

On that particular day, we were into problems clear up to our necks. For one thing, we had taken a lease on a building and then found out there was no way we were going to be able to use it. I was glad Mark had already eaten his lunch that day, because all he had for dessert was a whole dishful of trouble. We started serving it to him almost before he sat down, but he just sat there, taking it all in very calmly and smiling to himself.

When we finally ran out of words, he just said, "I think we can handle it," and he's been handling it ever since. We no longer have to be concerned about a thing. Mark showed us how to arrange our schedules and take care of our finances—even how to get along with each other. He took care of the building problem and found just the right place for us. He straightened out the whole mess we were in, put our affairs on a smooth-running basis, and he's been keeping it that way ever since.

Before long, I was getting invitations from many other churches to come and give my testimony. Then Rex Humbard asked me to be his guest on "Cathedral of Tomorrow," and after that, invitations started coming in from other states as well.

The Lord said that in the last days, He would pour out His spirit, and I never dreamed that He would pick somebody like me to witness to it, but He has. We're on the move all the time, and everywhere we go, I can see the mighty outpouring of His spirit and watch hundreds and hundreds of people coming to Him. You don't read about this in the newspapers. You have to be there in person to see it happening and feel it to the depth of your soul. But it's real, and it's happening all over the world!

I became involved with Richard Shakarian and his Youth Crusades, and that's when I realized that God had a special ministry for me. Richard made it possible for me to get the first new car I'd had since my Continental was stolen. I called it "Gracie," because it was truly given to me by the grace of God.

The Youth Crusades were held all over the country, and we went to Portland, Honolulu—everywhere. I sang with Andre Crouch and Barry McGuire and lots of well-known evangelists, but I knew that out there in that sea of young faces there were kids who needed to hear what I had to tell them. The first time I looked out at those thousands of kids who were sitting there waiting for us to go on, I knew that some of those kids were teetering on the edge of drugs, playing with the idea of "just trying it once" or experimenting in other ways.

That's when I went into my dressing room and got down on my knees and "grabbed God by the coattail." *Tell them what they need to hear,* I prayed. *Say it through me! Help me to get myself out of the way, so You can jerk them to their senses and keep them from ever getting involved with drugs. Show them how curiosity and the taunts and jibes of those who are already hooked will carry them over the brink to destruction. Help them to find Your Son, so they'll have Someone to hang onto in their hour of temptation.*

I've prayed like that ever since, every time I have a chance to talk to young people, whether it's one or two or ten thousand. And after I've prayed, I tell them how I let drugs ruin my life and how nothing but the grace of God could bring me out of it to where I am today.

There's a big movement on to decriminalize marijuana so you can't get into trouble with the law for smoking it. Well, let me tell you, you can get into trouble with your own mind and your own body and your own soul by smoking it. Lots of doctors are trying to say that it won't hurt you, that they even use it medicinally to calm people down and help them to breathe when they have asthma attacks.

Maybe it is helpful in those cases. Maybe it won't hurt you physically, but I know the devil uses it as a tool. He lulls your senses with it and keeps you from being awake and aware to the pitfalls he's putting in your path. People have gotten high on marijuana and have smashed up cars and killed themselves and other people. It lowers your resistance to alcohol, sex, and other drugs, and before you ever know what's happening, you're in over your head. I *know*—because I let it happen to me. *I was there* and only an act of God could get me out of it.

Don't let the devil get hold of you. Don't even take that first puff. You'll take another and another and another. Then you'll start using other things—uppers and downers, acid, and hard drugs—and you'll get hooked. And it will take everything you have away from you. It'll take your money; it will take your friends; it will take your home, your possessions, your self-respect, your ambitions; finally, it will take your life.

The Lord reached down into the awful mess I had made of my life, and He pulled me up and saved me. He delivered me from drugs and I praise Him constantly because I'm *free!* But I've had to stand by and see a lot of my friends destroyed and even murdered by drugs.

Not all of my former friends dropped away after I started going to church. Kelly and Sharon and most of the kids I had known at the Home still came around from time to time; but especially Kelly and Sharon. I never pressured them about giving their lives to Jesus, but I knew the difference in me was having an effect on them. I knew that Sharon especially wanted to give up her old life, because she told me so, but she didn't know how. Bartending and letting men "keep" her were the only things she knew, and she was afraid she couldn't make a living if she turned completely away from all that.

"I could wait on tables or do almost anything if I only had myself to think about," she used to tell me, "but I've got to think about my girls. It takes a lot of money to put two girls through high school, and I can't expect my mother-in-law to support them."

I kept assuring her that God would take care of her and them if she'd just give Him a chance, but she wasn't quite ready for that. I knew she wanted desperately to get off drugs too, and the fact that I had come off them cold—with absolutely no pain or difficulty of any kind—moved her deeply.

In December of that year, I went to Jerusalem and took "my Claudine"—my precious grandmother—with me. Being there in the Holy Land, seeing the places where Jesus walked and taught, was a memorable experience. But the greatest joy, for me, was that of seeing my beloved grandmother give her life to her Lord on Christmas Day in Bethlehem.

When we returned from that trip, I learned that while we had been visiting Jesus' birthplace, the devil had been busy at home. On December fifteenth, Sharon had been found dead in her apartment. She had been brutally mistreated, then hanged, and the police tried to dispose of the case neatly by calling it suicide, but I know better. Sharon would never have hanged herself, and there was no way that she could batter and abuse her body as it had been treated.

Several times, when she had been down, she had gone through the motions of suicide, but hanging was not Sharon's way. Her way was to get herself all made up as beautifully as she possibly could, then put on her most ethereal-looking negligee. Then she would take a heavy dose of sleeping pills, lay down on the couch, and just go to sleep. She would look like a sleeping princess, and if she had had a death wish, then it must have been mixed up in some way with the Sleeping Beauty fairy tale. But she had never had a chance to find out if death's kiss would awaken her into the land of "happily ever after," because I or someone else always found her and brought her around.

This death had been ugly and brutal, and I would never see her again. She had been my closest, dearest friend—warm, loving, giving, and faithful. She never left my side in my times of trouble and need, and I still hurt when I think of her.

I knew Sharon had been murdered because of drugs. I don't know just how, but I know drugs were the cause in some way.

These are the things I tell all those wide-eyed kids who come to our Youth Crusades and everywhere else when I'm speaking. When I tell them that drugs will take everything they have—their money, their possessions, their friends, and finally their lives—I know what I'm talking about. I have the scars on my heart to prove it.

It has taken me a few years to realize that God was listening, there in the hospital, the day I promised Him I'd live my life for Him, go where He wanted me to go, and do what He wanted me to do if He'd just make my baby well. But since I've been trying to keep my part of that bargain, He has never—for one moment—let me down.

Take the matter of finances, for example. It was slow and very wobbly going for me to "step out on faith." I had given my testimony at a few churches and I had seen what God could do by way of collection baskets, but when my unemployment insurance ran out I panicked. So the first thing I did was reach for the phone to call Brother Howard. He was used to it, by now. Ever since the day I had given my heart to Jesus right there on the carpet in his study, I had leaned on Brother Howard every time the going got rough.

When the search warrants were out for my arrest during the drug trials, when the devil piled high the temptation to take a couple of tranquilizers, when Damon got sick, when the bill collectors came around—just any excuse at all—I cried to him about it on the telephone or in person, even when I *knew* that all I was ever going to hear was his one and only pat answer for everything—"God will take care of it." Of course, God always did, but right in the thick of the trouble that answer sometimes sounded so downright trite!

It was Sunday morning, and I was down to my last twenty-dollar bill. I wanted to talk to him for just a few minutes right after church and ask him what I should do. Then I thought, but I already *know* what he'll say so what's the use of bothering him. "God will take care of it." Okay! How about letting God handle this one without involving the middleman.

But while I was waiting for Diane to pick me up on her way to church, I opened the Bible just to see what God would say. Well, there it was, my eyes followed down the page and rested on this: Malachi 3:10: "Bring all the tithes into the storehouse so that there will be food enough in my Temple; if you do, I will open up the windows of heaven for you and pour out a blessing so great you won't have room enough to take it in! Try it! Let me prove it to you!" (LB).

We went to church, and Diane and I took our places in the choir. When the collection plate was passed around, I took my twenty-dollar bill and held it in my hand inside my pocket. God and I had an argument about it right there in church.

"Put it in the plate," God said.

"Now wait a minute, Lord," I said. "I know I'm supposed to trust You. I know You're the giver of all gifts and the supplier of all my needs, but Lord, *this is all the money I have!"*

"Put it in the plate," God said again.

"But what am I going to do about groceries?" I asked. "You know I don't have any food in the house, and You know I don't have any milk for Damon, either. And this is positively my last twenty-dollar bill!"

"Put it in the plate!"

By that time the plate was being passed right down the row toward me, so I dropped the bill into it and said, "Praise the Lord." Then I thought, what am I praising the Lord for? There goes my very last cent!

But God has said, "I will supply all of your needs according to my riches in glory through Christ Jesus" (*see* Phillipians 4:19). I'm not just sure what that means or how much is involved, but I do know that God can never run out of anything. He is the Creator, the Author of everything that is, and all He needs to do is just make some more.

Diane and I were inching our way through the crowd on our way to the parking lot when this precious little man came up beside me and grabbed my arm. "God bless you, LuLu," he said and shoved a piece of paper into my hand. In a minute, he had shuffled away into the crowd, but when I got out into the parking lot, I looked at the paper, expecting to find some kind of note. Instead, it was a twenty-dollar bill.

Sometimes, He leads me right down to the last penny, but He has never left me penniless. Whenever I've come right down to the wire to pay a bill, or when I need groceries or gas for my car or any other kind of need, God has *always* supplied out of His riches. I get scared sometimes; I get shaky and filled with doubt and uncertainty. But when I look back, I can see that He has *never* failed me, and it strengthens my faith for one more time.

15

Struggle, a Necessary Part of Growth

There was something else that God took care of in His own time and His own way also.

Hundreds of times, when I have been in a restaurant or a supermarket or just waiting to have gas put in my car at a filling station, people have come up and asked for my autograph. I used to think, *Wow! If they can remember me for all those silly things I used to do on "Hee Haw," just think what I could tell them now!* I didn't think I could get back on the program. In fact, I didn't even have any idea of trying, but God took care of that, too.

One day I had a call from the now late Kathryn Kuhlman. She wanted me to come out to California to be on her television program, so Diane and I flew out. We went to the CBS Studios in Hollywood and talked over the things I was going to say and the songs I would sing on her program at the television studio next day. After that Diane and I had the rest of the day to ourselves.

"You know," I told her, "I haven't been in California since that first taping I did for 'Hee Haw.' Their production offices aren't very far from here. I have a good notion to go and see those people and tell them how the Lord has saved me and delivered me from drugs and how He's changed me."

"They can *see* how He's changed you," Diane said.

"Yeah, probably so," I said. "Maybe they won't even know me."

We walked into their offices and were greeted by a receptionist I hadn't seen before. I asked, "Is Marcia around?" and just then she walked through the door with some papers in her hand and said, "Hello. Can I help you?" She was looking at me, strangely, and I realized that she really *didn't* know me.

I said, "Hello, Marcia," and she recognized the voice at least.

"LuLu?" she said. "My goodness! It *is* you, LuLu. What's happened to you? You're so pretty! You don't even look like the same person!" Then she was embarrassed for what that implied.

She took me in to the producer's office, and we went through it all over again. "You don't even look like the same person," he said.

"I am *not* the same person," I told them. So I told them how I happened to be in California and that I had come up to see them and let them know how much I appreciated the fact that they had tried to help me. I said that everything was going fine for me now, and I just wanted to let them know. Then I poured it all out—how the Lord had saved me and set me on my feet and given me a ministry for Him. I told them about being completely off drugs and how grateful I was and how I was trying to help young people to get off drugs too or stay off if they weren't already hooked.

I said, "I want to thank you for all you did for me while I was on 'Hee Haw,' but it doesn't matter whether I ever get back on the program or not, because all I really want to do with my life from now on is work for Jesus. You know something?" I said, "He has even given me a voice. I can actually sing!"

So I sang "Amazing Grace" for them, and when I got through, they were in tears. This was definitely *not* the LuLu they had known! Not one swearword in the whole recitation. Soft spoken, ladylike—the coarse and cursing LuLu had completely disappeared.

The producer said, "I just can't believe it! You're so different. There seems to be a glow about you. I can really tell that something's happened to you."

By the time we were getting ready to go, they were talking about the possibility of having me back on the show. "Do you think you could come back?'' he asked.

I said, ''I don't really know. If the Lord opens the door for me, then, yes, I would like to come back. I'd like to be able to sing for Jesus on that program.''

He said, ''Well, we'll have to think about that. There's some things that would have to be resolved first, but it would be good to have you back.''

We went home, and I put the whole thing out of my mind, but a couple of months later there came a telephone call one day. It was the producer. ''We're going to Nashville to start taping on the third of next month,'' he said, ''and we want you to come back on the program.''

''Do I get to sing my gospel music?'' I asked.

''Yes,'' he said, ''we've agreed to let you sing one song.''

I was ecstatic. I went whooping and wheeing around the place, but poor little Damon didn't know what to make of it. Then I called Diane and shouted and screamed it all to her on the phone.

''Calm down, Lu,'' she said, ''you're talking so loud I can't hear a word you're saying!''

I was so excited. I couldn't wait to get up to Nashville. I just went around all day praising the Lord. ''You did it, Jesus,'' I told Him. ''You got me back on the program. There's just no way I would ever have been able to get back on 'Hee Haw' by myself.''

Naturally I could use the money. The first and most important thing was my ministry, witnessing to the saving power of the Lord Jesus Christ whenever and wherever I could, but the goodwill-offering kind of financial arrangement was always a very iffy thing. For a long time, we couldn't buy anything—not even stationery or a typewriter—until we had the money in advance. Yes, being back on ''Hee Haw'' was certainly going to help.

When I did go back up there, they couldn't believe their eyes. I was definitely *not* the LuLu they remembered. I guess what impressed them most, though, was the fact that I didn't have the foul mouth anymore.

Then when I got up to sing, they were surprised again. ''You're going to sing?'' they said.

''Yeah,'' I said. ''I'm going to sing 'Blessed Assurance.' ''

"*'Blessed Assurance?'* " they said. "You're going to sing a hymn?"

"That's right," I said and when I began they got surprised all over again. They'd heard me sing a few times before, when others on the show were practicing, but all they had ever heard was that high, squeaky tremolo I'd had all my life. This was something different. I gave them the sound tracks, and the band began making the charts for their music. I was going to sing along with them, but when I opened my mouth and the first deep, rich notes came rolling out, they all just stopped playing.

"I didn't know you could sing like that!" someone said, and I said I never could.

"Well, what happened?" they asked. "Have you been taking lessons?"

"No," I said, "I met Jesus, and He's given me a new voice to tell His message and sing His praise."

What I didn't tell them was that the first time those tones came out of my mouth, I was just as surprised as they were. After I was saved, I wanted to sing for Jesus more than I wanted anything in the world.

One Sunday night I was driving home from church after having been very deeply moved by the service and the song that one of the women in the choir had sung as a solo. She sang, "Jesus, There's Something About That Name," and it had touched me so deeply that I desperately wanted to be able to sing like that.

As I came to a red light, I was weeping and praising the Lord. The window was down, so I just stuck my hand out of the window straight up into the air and prayed, "Lord Jesus, I love You so, and Father, if You don't do anything else for me, please let me sing for Jesus."

Well, after that I just took the step in faith and began to sing. I'm sure they all just sat there and shook their heads at first and probably thought, "Oh, bless her heart! She's trying to sing for Jesus!"

But after that baptism in the Holy Spirit that night when those women put their hands on my head and prayed for me and I suddenly heard myself speaking in a heavenly language, something else happened. Again I was driving along the street, this time in front of a Jack in the Box drive-in. I opened my mouth to sing "Allelujah," and suddenly there was this deep, full voice. I guess I reacted like a boy whose voice is changing. I snapped my head around to see who was singing. Then I realized that sound had come out of *me!* God had answered my prayer! He had baptized me in His precious Holy Spirit and had given me the gift of song! *Now,* I could sing for Jesus!

And I did! I drove around for half an hour or more, singing every hymn I could think of at the top of my lungs and praising the Lord and crying—sometimes all at once.

After that, I joined the choir at my own church, and whenever I went to other churches to speak, I included a song or two in my testimony to show what God has done for me.

I have never taken a lesson, and I don't practice either. I just open my mouth to sing for my Lord and the music comes rolling out.

And in addition to the voice, He has also given me a gift for writing songs—the words, at least—and a precious friend who sets them to music.

One of the activities at Beverly Hills Baptist Church that I was very much interested in was the prison ministry. I had heard Johnny Cash a few times, and I thought if he could influence people out of his experience, then perhaps there was a way the Lord could use me, too.

There were a lot of people behind bars for the very same things I'd been mixed up in. I knew where they were coming from in their thinking, and I was sure it would help if I could tell them what the Lord had done for me.

There was a combo with a number of people who sang and played instruments, and they had a regular schedule of prisons that they visited, so I planned to go along on the next trip. I was still being dragged into court at that time because my case had not been settled. The next trip was going to be to the women's prison where I would go if I was sentenced.

Some of the folks went in the church bus. Diane and Paula got into my car with me, and we all drove up there in a sort of caravan. We parked where we were told to, and then we all walked to a guard station where they looked through our purses and wallets and passed a metal detector all over us. Then we all went out and stood in front of a huge iron gate. The guard pressed a button, and the gate opened, and we went through. I felt a shiver go all through me when that big gate clanged shut behind us and another one when we went through the second gate.

We went into a waiting room where there were two more guards who took our purses away and then led us into a large gymnasium with a stage and a basketball court. There were about 250 chairs set up on the gym floor, and there was a girl in every one.

I don't believe I've ever been in a colder place in my whole life. Not physically, because it was actually a pretty warm day, but the hostility was so icy it froze your soul.

Those girls just sat there in a sullen, dark brown mood, staring at the ceiling, their fingernails, or the backs of the girls in front of them. Not one of them would make eye contact with us.

The combo struck up a fast, bouncy number and some of the girls started keeping time with their feet, but when it was over, their applause was sarcastic. Did you ever hear people clap their hands so it sounded like a sneer? Those girls could do it.

Then one of the girls in our group, Julie, sang a solo and gave her testimony. Poor Julie! She was just so sweet, and she meant so well, but it went over like a lead balloon. She lived in a completely different world from these girls having been brought up in a nice, Christian atmosphere—Sunday school, church, the whole bit. Probably the greatest sin she ever committed in her nineteen years was swiping her mother's lipstick.

One by one, we went through all the numbers on our program, and then it was my turn. I had asked to be last, because I had a feeling that when I was through, we were either going to make a difference in a lot of lives or we were going to have to get out of there—fast!

I knew I could talk to those girls if I could just get their attention. I knew their language. I had lived in the same snarling, snapping jungle most of them had come from. I knew I could tell them what they needed to hear, but for the life of me, I didn't know how to begin.

When we went to the churches and youth rallies, I always

started out by telling about the Home. Ha! For most of these kids, the Home with all of its discipline and strictness would have seemed like heaven. At least at the Home we had clean beds to sleep in and clean clothes to wear and always enough to eat. And we never knew what it meant to be raped, either. No! I could hardly expect any sympathy from these girls for my living at the Home.

I went to the front of the platform and started adjusting the mike, and the Lord just opened it all up for me. A girl way up in the back called out, "Hi, LuLu. We know who you are. You've got plenty of friends in here!"

"I know I do," I answered back, "and don't be surprised if you wake up some morning and find me in a cell with you, too. I've had a coupla drug busts, you know, and the courts still haven't decided my case. But if I do come up here, I'm going to be praising God every day, because even if I do have to serve time, I'm *free* from the things that caused me to serve it.

"Let me show you what I mean. I've been a dopie like some of you. For a long time I was freaked out on acid every day of my life. Even the cops called me the biggest acid eater in town! I tried to take my own life, and my dearest friend hit me with speed to pull me out of it. She thought she was doing me a favor, but I was hooked. I had to have a hit of speed every day. My arms were so full of holes that there wasn't any place left to put the needle. My veins blew up, and I was shooting the stuff into the back of my hand.

"Look!" I said, pushing back my sleeves. "Can you see the marks? No you can't! Not even one of them, and you know why? Because Jesus took them all away. He healed me, and not only of drugs. He healed me of hate and defiance and a foul mouth and every loathsome thing that was in my heart. And you know something else? The day after I put my life into His keeping, I went all day long without my usual hit of speed *and I didn't even realize it!* And I've never needed it again! He took me off it cold—without one pain or twitch or shiver. *And He can do the same thing for you!"*

I pointed out Diane and Paula to them and told how they had taken me to church, time after time, and how the Lord finally got through to me. I told them about how I cussed out the pastor and then ended up on the floor of his study on my knees, pouring out my heart to Jesus.

Before I got through, one of the girls right in front broke down sobbing and then another and another. A little redheaded girl stood up and said, "You ain't coming to jail, LuLu, we're all gonna be prayin' for you."

Then a beautiful black girl stood up and started to sing, "Precious Lord Take My Hand." The combo found her key and followed along, and when they were through, all of us on stage were crying.

I had seen lots of people come down and give their hearts to the Lord when the altar call was given, but I had never seen the Lord work so powerfully as He did in that prison. Before we left there, we saw demons cast out; we saw people get filled with the Holy Spirit, and we saw a whole crowd of those girls who had never had a thing to do with Jesus come down front and put their lives in His hands.

I had never been higher than I was when we left there. All the way back, we were singing and praising the Lord as we drove along—right up until we got just three blocks from home. Suddenly, right in front of us, a sports car pulled out from the curb without any warning and crashed into the side of my car.

Whew! I was absolutely furious! All the hateful things I'd ever felt in my life came boiling up to the surface again. Maybe I thought all that was dead and buried, but it sure had a hasty resurrection! I piled out of the car and screamed out everything I could think of. My brand-new car! I'd only had it a short time and—up until then—there hadn't been a scratch on it. Now there was this ugly dent in the side.

We really had it out! By the time we got down to practical things like insurance and what I'd have to do to have my car fixed, it was quite a bit later. When I got back into the car, there were Diane and Paula just staring at me. "The air was getting a little heavy out there," Diane said quietly. "I thought I'd better roll up the window."

I felt so ashamed! Here I was, a born-again Christian, behaving like the toughest mule skinner that ever lived. We drove the rest of the way in silence, but I was reviling myself every turn of the wheel. And I'd just told those girls up at the prison that the Lord had delivered me from all of that. Well, the temper was still there, that was one thing for sure, and I hadn't really gotten rid of the foul language either.

So the next afternoon I went over to see Brother Howard, and I told him what had happened. "I thought I was born again," I told him. "I thought the Lord had taken away all that stuff and that now I was a new person in Him. Does this mean that I'm not really born again after all?"

"No," he laughed, taking off his glasses and rubbing his nose. "It only means that you haven't grown up yet. You see, LuLu, being born again is a great deal like being born the first time. It means that the Christ nature has been born in us, but it's a new, weak little nature just as we were new, weak little creatures when we came from our mothers' wombs. Actually, being born again means that we now have two natures.

"The old Adamic nature came right home from the hospital with us. As we got bigger and stronger, it grew bigger and stronger, too. The Adamic nature is our carnal nature. It controls and rules us. It is the separate ego, the material or earthly self. It doesn't put God first; it puts self first. It wants everything for itself.

"Even a tiny baby wants everything for itself. It cries for food, for attention, for cuddling. We grow up with that nature. Then one day we repent of our sins and we say, 'Jesus, come into my heart.'

"Now, when you did that did you suddenly feel the old nature just go swish and leave you? Uh uh! It's still there. But you *did* feel a new nature come into your heart, the nature of Christ. It was not big and strong like the Adamic nature. It was new and little and weak. And so this new weak little Christ nature gets battered and pushed around by the old Adamic nature until it grows big enough and strong enough to fight back. And when it does, then there is this constant warfare inside between the old Adamic nature and the new spiritual nature.

"We all want victory over the Adamic nature, but you know there is never a victory without some kind of fight. We *have* to struggle. We have to push and shove and get our noses rubbed into the dirt until we get big enough and our muscles get strong enough so we can win our battles.

"Our new nature has to be nurtured, encouraged, and protected so it can grow, too. We feed it by feeding on God's Word, by meditating on His teachings and His promises. Our spiritual muscles grow stronger every time we flex them in battle. The more we ignore that old Adamic nature, the more we turn away from it and stop feeding it with the 'I wants' and the I, me, and mine of life, the sooner it will starve and grow weaker and weaker and weaker.

"But remember, there can be a resurrection of that old nature, too. You may think it's dead just because you've won a battle or two and then all of a sudden, wham! There it is, alive, well, and kicking back at you again just when you thought it was completely beaten and buried. We go through battle after battle, over and over again.

"And sometimes in the midst of the struggle we wonder where is the victory? Where is the joy and the exultation I felt? But every time we win a victory over the old nature, we grow a little stronger, and we go a little longer before we have to do battle again.

"This is the excitement of the Christian life. This is the reason we're admonished and commanded in the Word of God to grow in grace and in the knowledge of our Lord Jesus Christ. This is the way that we become conformed to His image. Remember God's desire—His only desire for us—is that we be conformed, or made into, the image of His Son and that doesn't come without struggle."

As always, I left there feeling ten feet tall and floating on a cloud. It was a funny thing, but I had literally spent thousands and thousands of dollars to get high on drugs and nothing I had ever shot or swallowed or puffed had ever made me feel like this. I had confidence, peace, assurance, well-being, joy, and exuberance, and no amount of money in all the world could buy even one little smidgen of that. I hadn't failed after all. I was growing!

The next morning, in quite a different way, along came another chapter in this lesson on struggle.

I had gone down to hang a load of wash out on the line and was starting back up the stairs when a flicker of motion caught my eye. I put down the clothes basket and went around the back of the steps to investigate, and there was that little brown bag that had come from inside the caterpillar. Only now something was trying to crawl out of it. I went closer, and I could see a small black head with two big shiny eyes and what looked like two tiny coils of thread beside them.

As I watched, it appeared to be struggling desperately to get out. Two or three times there was a kind of jerking motion, then it seemed to pause and rest. I watched it for a moment or two, but it just wasn't getting anywhere. "Oh, dear God, it's a butterfly. It's really a butterfly," I said aloud. But maybe it couldn't get out. Maybe it was stuck in that cocoon. Do butterflies ever need cesarean operations, I wondered. Finally, when it just didn't seem to be getting any further, I ran upstairs and got my manicure scissors. Then I ran down again and almost bumped into the Avon lady at the bottom of the steps.

"Hello," she said, "may I . . . ."

"Not now," I interrupted. "I have to help with a breech birth."

"You *what?*" she said, looking at the scissors.

"It's a butterfly," I explained, hurrying around in back of the steps. "It's stuck in the cocoon and can't get out."

"No *don't!*" she screamed, hurrying after me and grabbing my arm. "Wait a minute! Please listen to me!" I listened because I had to. She was still clutching my arm.

"When we lived in Illinois," she said, "I brought this cocoon into the house, and we kept it for several months. Then one day when I was sewing, the butterfly started to emerge. It struggled and struggled, and I thought the same thing you did. That it couldn't get out. So finally I picked up my embroidery scissors and slit the cocoon.

"Well the butterfly crawled out and hung there for a while. The antennae—those little black coils beside the eyes? They slowly unrolled and the butterfly just seemed to shiver a few times but nothing else happened. The wings never expanded; they just stayed all crumpled and crippled, and for all of its short lifetime, that beautiful thing just crawled. It sucked the nectar from the flowers we brought it, but it never flew.

"On the second day, I called my son's biology teacher at high school and told him the problem. 'It seems to be eating all right, and it crawls around everywhere, but it has never flown,' I said."

" 'It never will, Mrs. Joslin,' he told me. 'You see, that struggling you saw is a necessary part of the emergence process. It helps to force the blood into the wings and strengthen them so they can be lifted, fanned, and dried. When you slit open the sack, you prevented that from happening.' And then he said something else I've never forgotten. *Struggle is a necessary part of growth in everything from a blade of grass to a human soul.*"

There were tears in my eyes as well as hers when she finished. Saying something about coming back later, she went on her way and left me standing there. I don't know how long it was, but I watched *my* butterfly jerk and push and squeeze itself out of that silken sleeping bag, maybe one millimeter at a time.

At long last, a beautiful monarch butterfly with wet, folded wings, pulled itself free of the cocoon and clung there at the edge. Slowly the tiny black antennae uncoiled and stretched above the head. Then ever so slowly the wings started to stretch and expand. Tiny bit by tiny bit, they reached outward and upward, the lovely orange and black markings seeming to deepen into a rich velvety glow.

Very slowly those beautiful wings began to move, up and down in graceful arcs of motion. "Oh, praise God!" I said and stretched out my hand. A tiny, fairylike foot reached toward my finger, then another and soon it was walking regally toward my palm. For a moment it rested there and, sobbing with joy, I restrained an impulse to lift it to my cheek.

I don't know how long I stood there, a few moments or an hour. But eventually it walked to the end of my fingers, lifted slowly into the sunlight and fluttered to a nearby bush.

From upstairs, I heard Damon crying. I picked up the clothes basket and walked slowly up the stairs.

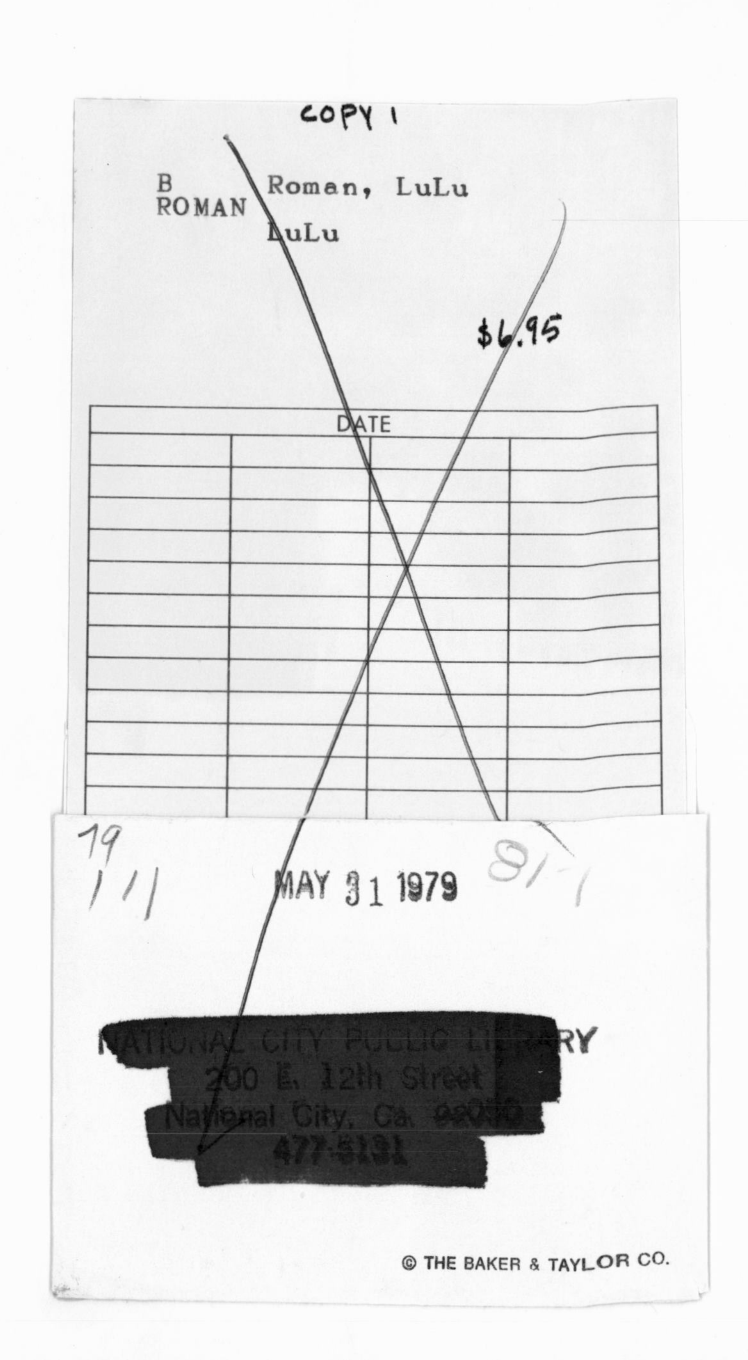
COPY 1
B
ROMAN
Roman, LuLu
LuLu
$6.95
DATE
19
1 1 1
MAY 31 1979
81-1
NATIONAL CITY PUBLIC LIBRARY
200 E. 12th Street
National City, Ca. 92050
477-5131
© THE BAKER & TAYLOR CO.